"This book provides the perfect answer to
engage in high-quality math discourse in my classroom?' The experiences of real
teachers in real classrooms, brought to life through a series of vignettes, provide vivid
illustrations of how the 11 techniques described can get students thinking and talking
about mathematics. The book is a game changer for elementary teachers!"

Margaret (Peg) Smith,
Emeritus Faculty, University of Pittsburgh

"We've come a long way since discussion in math class meant that individual
students shared their strategies one after the other with little interaction or reflection.
This book is based on the premise that discourse skills can and must be learned
and practiced if all students are to have access to participation in high-quality talk
about significant mathematical ideas. Based on a decade of work with teachers and
coaches, it provides clear, specific strategies illustrated with classroom examples for
supporting students as they learn how to talk, listen, and question during all phases
of the math lesson."

Susan Jo Russell,
Senior Researcher, TERC

"Packed with powerful teaching ideas—there are so many excellent teaching strategies
in this single book! A teacher could learn to implement one or two of these techniques
and the book will have been worth its cost. It provided ideas that I wanted to try to
implement RIGHT AWAY!"

Amanda Jansen,
Professor of Mathematics Education
University of Delaware

"This book does a great job of providing how-to steps that I was able to incorporate
into my own practice. These techniques for discourse are appropriate for a wide variety
of grade and skill levels. I especially appreciated the strategies for differentiation and
for meeting the needs of emergent multilinguals."

Tyler Erickson,
Fifth-Grade Teacher

"We teachers know students can talk. But teaching how to talk to further mathematical understanding is challenging. *Activating Math Talk* gave me strategies to guide students, even reticent ones, into meaningful mathematical discourse. It challenged me to be more purposeful in 'opening spaces for students to surprise you.' It changed the way I taught and listened to students, making me a better teacher, and helped me create an exciting, respectful classroom environment where my students gained confidence and competence in building shared mathematical understanding."

Kim Zeugner,
Elementary Teacher

"Fostering a discourse-rich classroom is essential for emergent multilingual learners to develop deep understandings of mathematics. The authors provide the what, why, and how of developing meaningful learning communities through practical, research-based suggestions that teachers can take directly into their classrooms. The inclusion of excerpts from real classrooms allows us insights into the teachers' and learners' experiences as we learn how to center and foster language in the mathematics classroom. This book is a great resource for teachers and teacher educators who wonder how to help move the math forward while students are acquiring language."

Zandra de Araujo,
Associate Professor of Mathematics Education,
University of Missouri

"This book is set up well for grade-level teams to do a book study and set goals for how they are working towards creating a discourse community in their classrooms."

Joshua Males,
K–12 Mathematics Curriculum Specialist

"This is a needed resource right now. We teachers just aren't doing this in our classrooms and we need a resource to develop this aspect of our instruction."

Kyle Cayce,
Elementary Teacher

Activating Math Talk: The Book at a Glance

This book is about purposeful and explicit math talk techniques for the elementary classroom that promote high-quality discourse school-wide. The techniques align to each phase of a lesson (launch, explore, discuss), and particular attention is paid to engaging emergent multilingual learners in math talk. In these pages you'll find the following useful features.

Figure I-2 • Math Discourse Matrix

		Correcting Discourse	**Eliciting Discourse**	**Probing Discourse**	**Responsive Discourse**
Discourse Dimensions	**Questioning**	1. T asks frequent, short-response questions that attend to Ss' accuracy and speed 2. T asks follow-up questions when needed to lead to correct answers 3. Ss ask T questions to establish correctness of answers	1. T asks open-ended questions that encourage many Ss to share their answers and how they found them, expanding the breadth of who participates 2. T asks follow-up questions to support the sharing and collection of several solutions 3. Ss ask T "what" and"how" questions to clarify solution methods	1. T asks probing questions that require Ss to justify their answer, how they found it, and why they used their approach 2. T asks follow-up questions to press for mathematical depth 3. Ss ask T "how" and"why" questions to clarify their own math thinking	1. T includes pressing questions that promote Ss sharing their answers, how, and why, and connections between math ideas and representations 2. T asks follow-up questions tocheck that all students are making sense of and connecting math ideas 3. Ss ask one another "how" and"why" questions, taking responsibility for understanding others' math thinking
	Explaining	1. T demonstrates procedures used to solve a problem 2. Ss present their answers when T asks 3. T praises correct answers and corrects Ss' incorrect answers	1. T adds to Ss' presentations of their solution methods for solving a problem 2. Ss present their answers and how they found them when T asks 3. T accepts incorrect and less sophisticated answers as indication of Ss' current understanding	1. T revoices and extends Ss' presentations of various solution methods for solving a problem 2. Ss presenttheir answers, how they found them, and why they approached a problem as they did when T or other Ss probe 3. T probes Ss' thinking about incorrect answers to deepen discussion about why they are incorrect	1. Ss restate, extend, and make connections across various solution methods presented 2. Ss volunteer their answers, how they found them, why they approached a problem as they did, and connections to other ideas 3. T and Ss examine incorrect answers so that *all* Ss can learn from mistakes and connect them to correct solutions
	Listening	1. T listens for correct answers to problems and proper vocabulary 2. Ss listen for T's verification of their answers	1. T listens for Ss' answers and how they found them, with attention to Ss' vocabulary 2. Ss listen for T's reactions to ensure they have an acceptable procedure	1. T listens for Ss' explanation of their answer and rationale, with attention to Ss' vocabulary 2. Ss listen to others'explanations to consider if their ideas are similar	1. T listens for partial and complete understanding in Ss' explanations and connections, with attention to Ss' vocabulary 2. Ss listen to others' explanations to make connections across math ideas
	Modes of Communication	1. T and Ss communicate in T-S-T patterns 2. T favors the use of verbal or pictorial modes when T/Ss share procedures and answers 3. T provides Ss with representations they need to use to solve a problem 4. T favors Ss' use of academic language as "correct"; first or everyday language, if permitted, lacks math connections	1. T and Ss communicate in T-S-T-S patterns 2. T makes verbal, pictorial, or written modes available as Ss communicate the answer and how they got it 3. T accepts all representations as equally effective 4. T allows Ss' use of academic, first, and everyday languages equally as modes to share answers and methods	1. T and Ss communicate in T-S-T-S or T-S1-S2-S3 patterns 2. T encourages use of multiple modes as Ss share ananswer, how they got it, and why they used their approach 3. T encourages Ss' use of various representations to convey math thinking 4. T encourages Ss' use of academic, first, and everyday languages when appropriate to convey math meaning	1. T and Ss communicate with significant S-S patterns 2. T requires use of multiple modes of communication as Ss share the answer, how they got it, why, and math connections 3. T expects comparisons across representations to develop math understanding 4. T expects use of academic, first, and everyday languages to develop math understanding

Discourse Types

← Difference in Breadth →   ← Difference in Depth →   ← Difference in Responsibility →

Source: Project All Included in Mathematics, North Carolina State University and Horizon Research, Inc. Copyright 2020. Used with permission.

The Math Discourse Matrix describes the qualities of four discourse types and what teachers and students do in each.

Throughout the book, find definitions of key terms and opportunities to consider how key points or nuances relate to your own instruction.

math is defined as including "purposeful exchange of ideas through classroom discussion, as well as through other forms of verbal, visual, and written communication" (p. 29). Students have opportunities to express ideas, clarify meaning, construct arguments, and compare approaches to build shared understanding of math concepts as well as flexibility with procedures.

In our work, we think of math discourse as *patterned ways of using questioning, explaining, listening, and different modes of communication in the classroom to promote conceptual understanding in math for all learners.*

Because each part of the math discourse definition is important, we like to break it down. Let's start with *patterned*. Classroom discourse is not about the way teachers do something one day or for a few cool lessons. Discourse is created out of the overall structures teachers put in place every day, sometimes without saying anything. Students learn how to participate from what teachers emphasize is valuable.

Math discourse: patterned ways of using questioning, explaining, listening, and different modes of communication in the classroom to promote conceptual understanding in math for all learners

THINK ABOUT IT

Think about the proposed definition for math discourse.

What are existing conversation patterns in your math classroom? What do these patterns mean to you when it comes to helping your students learn mathematics?

Consider the following two tasks.

Task 3-1	Task 3-2
Mr. Gayles is building a rectangular school garden with two 5-foot sides and two 7-foot sides. What is the perimeter of the garden?	The perimeter of the rectangular school garden Ms. Guilford is building is 24 feet. What are the possible dimensions of the garden?

Figure 3-1 • Does Your Task Promote or Limit Discourse?

DISCOURSE-PROMOTING TASKS	DISCOURSE-LIMITING TASKS
• Require cognitive effort due to the newness or the unpredictable nature of the solution • Require examination of task context that may limit or expand possible solution strategies and solutions • Require access to relevant knowledge and experiences to work through the task • Require examination of the nature of mathematical concepts, processes, and relations • Require complex and nonalgorithmic thinking • Require multiple representations and connections among representations	• Require a focus on the answer with attention to its correctness instead of its processes • Require no explanation or explanation focused solely on definitions and procedure without relevance to context • Require reproducing previously learned facts, rules, or formulae • Require no connection to concepts or meaning that underlie definitions or procedures • Require little cognitive demand beyond use of the procedure called for • Require one specifically called-for representation

Source: Adapted from Smith and Stein (1998).

Learn how to analyze how well your math tasks promote or limit math discourse, and find many examples of high-quality tasks.

Examine Practice scenarios provide opportunities to analyze and reflect on the implementation of talk techniques in authentic elementary classrooms.

EXAMINE PRACTICE

Read the following vignette from Ms. Ladeaux's classroom, where Story Problem Retelling is used two times during the Launch phase of a lesson. What purposes might Ms. Ladeaux have for each use of the technique?

Story Problem Retelling in Ms. Ladeaux's Kindergarten Classroom

Planning the Lesson

After 13 years teaching first grade, I am in my first year teaching Kindergarten. My story shares my experience launching a lesson on addition and subtraction within 10 using Story Problem Retelling. My class had been exploring the idea that adding or subtracting 1 gives the next, or the prior, number on the counting sequence. We also worked with adding or subtracting 2. So in this lesson I wanted to build on that learning as we worked with bigger numbers within 10. My math goal was for students to realize there are many strategies they can use to solve addition or subtraction problems within 10.

SIGNS OF SUCCESS

- Students use prior knowledge as an asset to make their predictions.

- Students listen carefully to each other's predictions.

- Students' bets contribute to the mathematical understanding of the problem.

- Students analyze predictions using the two key questions.

CAUTION SIGNALS

- Students make predictions that are unrelated to the problem or only about the context. (Use the "What new mathematical information" question to point out this limitation.)

- Students focus only on guessing what the problem will say, not on what makes an appropriate prediction. (Remind students what makes a prediction mathematically productive.)

Signs of Success and Caution Signals highlight indicators of successful technique implementation and foreshadow potential challenges that might arise.

Key Takeaways help summarize the most salient points from each lesson phase.

KEY TAKEAWAYS ABOUT THE LAUNCH PHASE

Part III presented three talk techniques for the Launch—Story Problem Retelling, Task Think-Aloud, and Math Bet Lines—and their accompanying classroom vignettes. These chapters illustrated teachers attending to different purposes in the Launch to prepare students for productive engagement with math content and in mathematical discussions. Here are the main takeaways from these chapters:

- Use the Launch techniques for specific purposes, and remember that techniques for techniques' sake do not change discourse.

- Set the tone for the work of the lesson with the Launch, and make sure your students can be successful in the subsequent Explore and Discuss phases.

- Do not use the Launch to tell students what to do, and avoid going so far with your Launch that there is little left for students to do or talk about.

DISCUSS WITH COLLEAGUES

1   How does your definition of math discourse compare to the definition provided in this chapter? Which of the four parts of the definition (patterned; using questioning, explaining, listening, and different modes of communication; conceptual understanding; for all learners) are easier for you to support in your classroom? Which are more challenging? Why?

2   Think about a math lesson you recently taught. Share what happened in this lesson with your colleagues using the discourse features from the Math Discourse Matrix (Figure I-2). What evidence from your classroom indicates the types of discourse you and your students engaged with during the lesson?

Discuss With Colleagues sections help you reflect on your practice as a team.

CONNECT TO YOUR PRACTICE

Pick one discourse dimension (questioning, explaining, listening, or modes of communication) under probing or responsive discourse. Plan and implement a math lesson focused on helping students engage in features of that particular dimension. Think about supports your students will need to engage in those ways. After your lesson, consider:

☐ How well did students engage in those features of the dimension? What was successful and what was challenging for students?

☐ What might you do differently in the future to improve student engagement in that dimension?

Connect to Your Practice sections give you opportunities to apply and reflect on a new skill.

ACTIVATING
Math
Talk

Grades
K–5

11 Purposeful Techniques
for Your Elementary Students

Paola Sztajn | Daniel Heck | Kristen Malzahn

CORWIN **Mathematics**

For information:

Corwin
A SAGE Company
2455 Teller Road
Thousand Oaks, California 91320
(800) 233-9936
www.corwin.com

SAGE Publications Ltd.
1 Oliver's Yard
55 City Road
London, EC1Y 1SP
United Kingdom

SAGE Publications India Pvt. Ltd.
B 1/I 1 Mohan Cooperative
Industrial Area
Mathura Road, New Delhi 110 044
India

SAGE Publications Asia-Pacific Pte.
Ltd.
18 Cross Street #10-10/11/12
China Square Central
Singapore 048423

Publisher, Mathematics: Erin Null
Development Editor: Desirée A. Bartlett
Editorial Assistant: Caroline Timmings
Production Editor: Tori Mirsadjadi
Copy Editor: Sarah J. Duffy
Typesetter: Integra
Proofreader: Liann Lech
Indexer: Integra
Cover Designer: Janet Kiesel
Marketing Manager: Margaret O'Connor

This material is based upon work supported by the National Science Foundation under Grant Nos. EHR-1513155, EHR-1513104 and EHR-1020177. Any opinions, findings and conclusions or recommendations expressed in this material are those of the author(s) and do not necessarily reflect the views of the National Science Foundation.

Printed in the United States of America.

Library of Congress Cataloging-in-Publication Data
Names: Sztajn, Paola, 1964-author. | Heck, Daniel J., author. | Malzahn, Kristen, author.
Title: Activating math talk : 11 purposeful techniques for your elementary students / by Paola Sztajn, Daniel Heck, and Kristen Malzahn.
Description: Thousand Oaks, California : Corwin, [2021] | Includes bibliographical references.
Identifiers: LCCN 2020023635 | ISBN 9781544394305 (paperback) | ISBN 9781071821602 (adobe pdf) | ISBN 9781071821572 (epub) | ISBN 9781071821596 (epub)
Subjects: LCSH: Mathematics—Study and teaching (Elementary) | Forums (Discussion and debate) | Discussion.
Classification: LCC QA20.F67 .S98 2021 | DDC 372.7—dc23
LC record available at https://lccn.loc.gov/2020023635
This book is printed on acid-free paper.

SUSTAINABLE FORESTRY INITIATIVE
Certified Chain of Custody
Promoting Sustainable Forestry
www.sfiprogram.org
SFI-01268

20 21 22 23 24 10 9 8 7 6 5 4 3 2 1

Contents

PART I: UNDERSTANDING HIGH-QUALITY MATH DISCOURSE FOR ALL STUDENTS

PART II: ACTIVATING MATH DISCOURSE IN THE CLASSROOM

PART III: TALK TECHNIQUES FOR THE LAUNCH PHASE

PART IV: TALK TECHNIQUES FOR THE EXPLORE PHASE

PART V: TALK TECHNIQUES FOR THE DISCUSS PHASE

PART VI: PUTTING IT ALL TOGETHER

CHAPTER 17: PLANNING AND REFLECTING TO PROMOTE HIGH-QUALITY DISCOURSE

Acknowledgments

For over 10 years, our team has been conceptualizing, executing, and researching the ideas that are now part of this book. This work on promoting high-quality discourse in elementary classrooms has been generously supported by a number of grants from the National Science Foundation[1] and has involved colleagues at North Carolina State University (NC State), Horizon Research, Inc. (HRI), and several partner districts. We cannot start this acknowledgment without thanking all of them for their incredible dedication to education, their support of this initiative, and their friendly critique, always pushing our work forward. From the NC State team over the years, we want to thank Steve Amendum, Lara Dick, Angela Klipsch, Ellen McIntyre, Bonnie Melton, Tina Starling, Mona Tauber, Christine Taylor, Aaron Trocki, Patricia Vargas, Temple Walkowiak, Tracy Foote White, and Angela Wiseman for all their contributions to the project. We also want to say a special thanks to Reema Alnizami and Anna Thorp not only for their support of our project, but for their specific contributions in helping us organize this book. Similarly, from the HRI team, we thank Kiira Lyons, Gwen Moffett, Jennifer Sprague, and Shayla Thomas for their work on the project, and we want to give special recognition to Michelle Blessing, Jessica Dula, Pippa Hoover, and Courtney Plumley for working with us and contributing to the writing of this book. Given our timeline for this ambitious project, we could not have completed this volume without their dedication and support.

Overall, this book is about and for teachers. In 10 years of our work with Project AIM (All Included in Mathematics), we have been privileged to have partnered with great districts and incredible elementary teachers. Our project moved from working with math coaches who piloted initial ideas for us all the way to a randomized trial, with many iterations of the program in between. Over 300 teachers have participated in our professional development across three partner districts, and we are very thankful to all of them. We have also been very fortunate to work with incredible district math coordinators and over 20 dedicated and professional math coaches.

---

1 The ideas presented in this book are based upon work supported by the National Science Foundation under Grants # 1021177, 1513104, and 1513155. Any opinions, findings, conclusions, or recommendations included are those of the authors and do not necessarily reflect the views of the National Science Foundation.

We cannot thank enough all teachers, coaches, and leaders who have joined us in Project AIM. You keep elementary mathematics education moving forward, every single day! What we have learned with you and from you in these past years has changed us and made us better mathematics educators. In particular, we want to highlight Suzette Acree, Megan Busick, Amy Long, Kristen Lucidi-Doty, Carol Mohn, Julie Schmidt, Elizabeth Scott, Jennifer Talton Sawyer, and Kim Zeugner for their contributions to our work. Thank you for your dedication to Project AIM.

We also want to thank our colleagues at NC State and HRI who have been patient with us as we shifted our attention to working on this book; our evaluators, Judy Storeygard, Jim Hammerman, and Mike Cassidy; several colleagues who have served as our national advisors throughout the life of Project AIM; Mandy Jansen for encouraging us to write a book sharing our ideas; and the team at Corwin who provided us with guidance: Erin Null, Desirée Bartlett, and Jessica Vidal. Each of you allowed us to bring this project to fruition. Finally, we want to thank our families, Russ, Joe, Clara, Jill, Rainie, Logan, Scott, and Ella for encouraging us to go after our professional goals and pursue this project from beginning to end. We spent many evenings and weekends away from you, and we appreciate your flexibility and kindness in enabling this important effort for us. Thank you!

PUBLISHER'S ACKNOWLEDGMENTS

Corwin gratefully acknowledges the contributions of the following individuals:

Amanda Allan, Mathematics Lecturer
University of Victoria
Victoria, BC, Canada

Tonya Bartell, Associate Professor of Mathematics Education
Michigan State University
East Lansing, MI

Victoria Bill, Resident Fellow, Research Associate
Institute for Learning, Learning Research and Development Center
Gibsonia, PA

Kyle Cayce, Elementary Teacher
Castro Valley, CA

Linda Davenport, Director of K–12 Mathematics
Boston Public Schools
West Roxbury, MA

Tyler Erickson, Fifth-Grade Teacher
Oaks Christian School
Westlake Village, CA

Kristine Klingensmith, Fellow
Institute for Learning, University of Pittsburgh
Penn Hills, PA

Amanda Jansen, Professor of Mathematics Education
University of Delaware
Newark, DE

Joshua Males, K–12 Mathematics Curriculum Specialist
Lincoln Public Schools
Lincoln, NE

Kristen Mangus, Math Support Teacher
Howard County Public School System
Columbia, MD

Cathy Martin, Executive Director, Curriculum and Instruction
Denver Public Schools
Denver, CO

Kateri Thunder, PreK Teacher, Math Division Lead
Charlottesville City Schools
Charlottesville, VA

About the Authors

Paola Sztajn is a professor of mathematics education at North Carolina State University and is a principal investigator in Project AIM (All Included in Mathematics). Her research program focuses on elementary teachers' professional development in mathematics and has been supported with several grants from different funding agencies. She has written over 90 papers, mostly focused on elementary school mathematics teachers and teaching. The overarching question guiding her 20+ years of work in mathematics education is: In which ways do practicing elementary teachers acquire and continue to develop the professional knowledge and identity needed to teach all students high-quality mathematics? She works with colleagues from different fields in collaborative studies that allow for in-depth investigations of this complex question.

Daniel Heck is vice president of Horizon Research, Inc. in Chapel Hill, North Carolina, and is a principal investigator in Project AIM. His research and development work spans many areas of mathematics education: classroom learning environments and discourse; teacher professional development design, enactment, and impacts; curriculum design and enactment; and student problem solving. Tying all of this work together is a central interest in how teaching and learning in school can tap into students' intuitions, informal ideas, and insights to develop powerful, formal understandings of mathematics. He has enjoyed and benefitted from collaboration with colleagues in practice and research locally, across the country, and around the world who share this interest.

Kristen Malzahn is a senior researcher at Horizon Research, Inc. in Chapel Hill, North Carolina, and a co–principal investigator in Project AIM. She began her career as an elementary school teacher and went on to receive an MEd in curriculum and instruction at the University of North Carolina at Greensboro. Over the past two decades, she has worked on several mathematics education research and evaluation projects and published a number of journal articles and book chapters, many of which focused on mathematics professional development for elementary and middle grades teachers. Understanding the many successes and challenges of teaching, she is most interested in supporting teachers as they work to provide effective mathematics instruction for every student.

Preface

SETTING THE STAGE: SUPPORTING MATH LEARNING THROUGH PRODUCTIVE TALK

Talk has been recognized as key to learning for quite some time, and research continues to demonstrate the importance of productive talk for learning math. Presenting and justifying one's reasoning, critiquing the arguments of others, and engaging in meaningful mathematical discussions are fundamental practices that support math learning. Further, listening, communicating, and collaborating are skills we want to instill in our students as they grow up to fully participate in a technological society. So engaging students in productive talk is a win-win investment in math classrooms.

Almost a decade ago, we started our work with elementary teachers to support them as they engaged their students in math talk. Three important principles guided our initial efforts and have continued to inform us over the years.

Principles That Guide Our Work

1. Practical techniques that can be readily and purposefully implemented help teachers build a toolkit for activating high-quality math discourse.
2. Techniques help students learn about important and specific aspects of math talk, building skills and dispositions for participating in high-quality math discourse.
3. All students can learn to participate productively in high-quality math discourse when they are provided opportunities with scaffolds to support their engagement; the techniques we share with teachers create these opportunities.

PURPOSEFUL TALK TECHNIQUES FOR THE ELEMENTARY CLASSROOM

Searching for practical techniques to support discourse, we partnered with colleagues in literacy education and identified techniques that could be adapted for math instruction. We developed a yearlong professional development program around these adapted techniques and worked with over 300 K–2 teachers. Their success with the program and implementation of the talk techniques in their classrooms encouraged us to share our work with elementary teachers more broadly. Teachers in our program learned to choose what technique to use when and for what purpose—something we emphasize, because techniques used for their own sake do not strengthen math lessons. Knowing when and why to use particular techniques is key, and in this book, we make the case for such purposeful use of talk techniques to activate and improve math discourse.

PROMOTING HIGH-QUALITY DISCOURSE SCHOOLWIDE

In addition to helping teachers think about their own teaching, we designed this book as a resource for promoting high-quality discourse schoolwide. The content of the chapters and discussion questions within them are meant to spark conversations among teachers, teacher leaders, and administrators about how to get kids talking about math in productive ways. Sharing these ideas with colleagues during professional learning opportunities can generate strong momentum at your school to improve the overall quality of discourse in math classrooms. Here are some suggestions for using this book to promote and nurture productive math talk schoolwide:

- **Professional learning community (PLC) book study:** Read and discuss this book during PLC meetings. Use the discussion questions at the end of each chapter as opportunities for application to practice and reflection.
- **Grade-level team planning:** Incorporate ideas and resources from the book into grade-level team planning to more purposefully plan for discourse.
- **Lesson study:** Use the lesson study process where teachers collaboratively plan, teach, observe, and debrief lessons aimed at high-quality discourse using talk techniques from the book.
- **Demonstration lessons:** Conduct demonstration math lessons that incorporate talk techniques and use the resources from the book to analyze the nature of student discourse that occurred and what supported or hindered it.
- **Classroom video analysis:** Analyze videos of teachers implementing talk techniques in the classroom, and discuss both the nature of the discourse that occurred and teacher moves that supported or hindered it (e.g., video clubs).

ORGANIZATION OF THIS BOOK

Parts I and II of this book provide important context and purpose to the techniques. Although you may be tempted to jump ahead to the technique chapters, we strongly encourage you to read Parts I and II first because they provide guidance to ground you in this work. The initial chapters help you consider what high-quality discourse looks like in math classrooms, how everyone participates, and what it takes to activate such talk. You'll also find suggestions for how to create a discourse community and how to plan your lessons to support robust math conversations. We pay deliberate attention to engaging all students, particularly emergent multilingual learners.

Parts III, IV, and V present the 11 talk techniques, organized by three phases of enacting a math lesson: Launch, Explore, and Discuss. The technique chapters also include vignettes from real classrooms illustrating the techniques in action. The book concludes with Part VI, which ties everything together and offers a lesson-planning tool to help you focus on purposeful planning and reflection when using the talk techniques in your instruction.

SUPPORTING FEATURES

To support professional learning and reflection on math discourse practices, we provide the following features in the chapters that invite you and your colleagues to explore the ideas presented and consider their application to your classroom instruction.

- **Definitions of key terms** in the margins
- **Think About It** moments to draw your attention to particular key points or nuances of practice and help you consider how they relate to your own instruction
- **Scenarios** that provide classroom examples of tasks and techniques
- **Signs of Success and Caution Signals** to highlight indicators of successful technique implementation and foreshadow potential challenges that might arise
- **Examine Practice** vignettes that provide opportunities to analyze and reflect on the implementation of talk techniques in authentic elementary classrooms; note, pseudonyms have been used for all teachers and students

- **Discuss With Colleagues** questions meant for group discussions to take stock of what you are reading and how it may impact math teaching and learning in your classrooms
- **Connect to Your Practice** activities for you to try in your own classroom and then reflect

Written in a friendly style with direct language that demystifies math talk and provides specific guidance for its implementation, this book is useful to a wide audience, from elementary school teachers, to leaders, to those interested in discourse or math instruction more broadly. It is the culmination of many years of work with teachers and leaders who have tested and vetted the ideas we share. As you get started, we encourage you not only to read the chapters in this book, but also to try the ideas in your practice and talk about them with your colleagues, because talk will help you learn!

Understanding High-Quality Math Discourse for All Students

What does it mean to activate math talk? Our work with teachers has shown us that the answer to this question varies tremendously. Part I introduces our vision of what high-quality math discourse means to us, and that vision guides everything in this book. In Part I we discuss the following:

- What constitutes high-quality math discourse (Chapter 1)
- What it means to activate high-quality discourse for *all* students, in particular emergent multilingual learners (Chapter 2)
- What teachers need to know mathematically to be able to activate high-quality discourse for *all* students (Chapter 3)

Starting with some definitions to establish important vocabulary, Part I sets the stage for the talk techniques presented later in this book. Keep in mind that techniques are meaningless unless used in service of wider goals. Part I sets the vision for these goals; as you start to read about and implement the techniques in your classroom, continue to come back to these introductory chapters for reflection. You will see that teachers who allow students to talk about math open a new door for math instruction! Kids have incredible ideas that can transform teaching. Focusing on what students say generates new excitement in teaching math, and having techniques to do so can make productive math talk a reality in the classroom.

High-Quality Discourse in Math Classrooms

Kids talk. In fact, most kids talk most of the time when among classmates or friends. Students of all ages, including young ones, are often not shy during recess or while playing on the playground. They talk in the classroom, and teachers often have to ask them not to talk during instructional time. So what's all the fuss about getting kids to talk in class and engaging them in discourse when learning math? Wouldn't it just be the case that if we let students talk, then math talk would flourish in the classroom?

Activating math talk is not that simple and actually not that natural. This book is based on the premise that students need to *learn to talk in specific ways* during math lessons for the talk to contribute to math learning—and this is especially true for young students. These ways of talking are different from how kids talk on the playground or in other subject areas. Thus, activating math talk is not just a matter of telling students to talk. Rather, participation in productive math conversations is a skill that is taught and learned.

COMPARING DISCOURSE SCENARIOS

To start thinking about math discourse, consider the following two fictional scenarios constructed to highlight some important points. In each scenario, the teacher is working with a second-grade class on the following problem:

> For all games at Poe Elementary School, students have to wear either blue or red shirts. There are 35 students in the gym for a game. If 16 are wearing red shirts, how many are wearing blue?

Students had time to think about the problem before the teacher initiated the discussion. As you read the scenarios, think about what makes the discourse in these classrooms similar or different. Consider what the teachers and the students are doing or saying in each classroom.

SCENARIO 1-1

Teacher: Who knows the answer? (About five students raise their hands immediately and the teacher points to one of them.)

Student 1: Nineteen.

Teacher: Great, how do you know?

Student 1: Because 35 minus 16 is 19.

Teacher: Great, and how do you know that?

Student 1: I wrote it down here on my paper. (Student shows the paper.) I cannot take 6 away from 5, so I cross out the 3 to make 15. I went 7, 8, 9, 10, 11, 12, 13, 14, 15. (Student tracks numbers counted with fingers.) That is 9, so I need 9 to go from 6 to 15. The 3 is now a 2. Now I have 2 take away 1 and that is 1. The answer is 19.

Teacher: Very good. Did everyone get that? (Teacher waits a couple of seconds and a handful of students nod their heads yes.) Anyone else? Any other way of doing this?

Student 2: I do not get it because I think it is 20. I just counted: 16, 17, 18, 19, . . . (student continues to count and show fingers to keep track of each number counted) 34, 35. See, I went over my hands twice and counted 20.

Teacher: You do not count the 16. You start at the 17 because you are counting the jumps. Very nice strategy! If you start at 17, you will count 19 numbers, so the answer is 19. Good strategy. Other ideas? (Teacher waits a little more.) Can someone explain to me the two solutions we have discussed?

Student 3: The first one is just like 35 minus 16, and we know that is 19. The second one is like, you start counting up from 16 to get to 35, and that is also 19.

Teacher: Exactly, two different ways to solve this problem. Very nice. Anyone else?

Student 4: I used blocks and also got 19.

Teacher: How did you use your blocks? Can you show our class?

Student 4: I got 3 blocks here and then 5 blocks to make 35. (Student shows tens and ones blocks and continues using the blocks throughout this explanation.) I have to separate 16. I take 1 ten and 5 ones because I have them. I still have 20, but I have to take 1 more away because it is 6 and not 5. If I take that one more now I have 19.

Teacher: Very good. You went from the left to the right, and took 1 from 3 first, but it worked with the blocks. Good work. Let's look at the next problem.

SCENARIO 1–2

Teacher: Who knows how to solve this problem? (About five students raise their hands immediately and the teacher waits until more hands go up.) Let me see . . . someone who has not yet shared today. (Teacher waits a little longer, a couple more hands go up, and teacher points to one of them.)

Student 1: I got 19.

Teacher: Can you explain the problem you were trying to solve and then how you got 19?

Student 1: I was trying to do 35 minus 16.

Teacher: Why were you trying to do that?

Student 1: Because 35 is like red and blues together. The students are blue or red and 16 are red. I am trying to find the blue ones.

Teacher: (Looking at the class.) What do you think about this idea that to find the blue shirts we need to take apart the 16 from 35?

Student 2: Can a student have a white shirt?

Student 1: I was thinking that students with wrong shirts are not in the gym. I was thinking the 35 students had a red shirt or a blue shirt. No other colors.

Student 3: If there are white shirts it is really hard. And what about other colors? That is confusing.

Teacher: Good point, so, in this problem, we are thinking the shirts are blue or red only. This is important. Let's hear the rest of the explanation. Why are you subtracting?

Student 1: I have to separate the 16 red from all students to see which ones are blue. So I wrote 35 minus 16 on my paper. (Student shows the paper.) I cannot take 6 away from 5, so I cross out the 3 and it is now 15.

Teacher: Let's stop here. Can you explain what you mean by you cannot take 6 away from 5?

Student 1: It is too many. I have to start with my ones and I am trying to subtract 6, but I only have 5 ones in the 35. So I have to get a ten from the 30 and make it into ones.

Student 4: Like if you had blocks.

Student 1: Yes, I ungrouped 1 ten and I have 2 tens and 15 ones. And I can now take 6 ones away. That is 9. And I can take 1 ten away, and I have 1 ten left, so 19 blue shirts left.

Teacher: Does anyone have a question about this solution?

Student 5: Could you trade all the tens?

Student 1: Hmm . . . I guess I could, but I only need to trade one of them and it is easier. I only need to subtract 6 ones.

Student 4: I added instead of subtracted, is that okay?

Teacher: What do you mean?

Student 4: I was adding to the 16. I added 10 and got to 26. Then I counted:

27, 28, . . . (student tracks numbers counted with fingers) 34, 35. That is 9. With the 10, I also got 19.

Student 6: I added too, but got 20. So 16, 17, . . . (student tracks numbers counted with fingers) 34, 35. That is 20 and not 19.

Student 4: You have to start with 17, because 16 is still red. Seventeen is the first blue shirt. Like if you lined them all up. Do you get it?

Student 6: Okay. If I start at 17, then I guess you are right, I get 19.

Teacher: Those of you who have not yet shared, what are you thinking?

Student 7: It looks like we have different ways and there are 19 students with blue shirts.

Teacher: What do you mean different ways?

Student 7: We can subtract, we can add tens and ones, or we can add all ones.

Teacher: Nice summary. Anyone else? When we add we are counting up, remember? (Points to one student who is quiet.) Can you summarize from the beginning?

Student 8: Hmm . . . there are 35 students in the gym. Sixteen have red shirts. We want to find out the blue shirts. There is like blue and red only. To find the blue, I can subtract 16 from 35 or count up from 16 to 35. If you count up, you start at 17. We get 19 blue shirts.

Student 9: I have another way to do it. I counted backward.

Teacher: That is great, and counting backward can also work—you can show me your way later. And can there be even some other ways to solve this? (Students nod yes.) I am sure there are a few other great ways. For today we will stop our discussion with that great summary because we need to move on to other topics, but we will come back to the counting backward strategy later this week.

Figure 1-1 lists a few features of the two scenarios that are important to consider when comparing the nature of the math talk happening. Check some of these against the ones you noticed regarding what the teachers and students were doing.

When thinking about different math classroom conversations, it is important to consider who is talking, who they are talking to, what is being talked about, and for what purposes. Are students explaining what they did, how, and why as part of their argument? Are they making connections across multiple ideas, procedures, or representations? Who is asking the questions, and what types of questions are they asking? Who is answering these questions?

THINK ABOUT IT

Compare and contrast Scenario 1-1 and Scenario 1-2.

What did you notice about the nature of math discourse in each scenario? How are they similar and different in terms of how students are participating in the discussion and what math they are learning? How are the teachers supporting the students?

learning
pit
when they can the
struggle explain the
the explain problem.

Figure I-I ◆ Comparing Discourse Scenarios

	SCENARIO I-I	SCENARIO I-2
TEACHER	• Includes more than one student in conversation. • Focuses on solving 35 – 16. • Asks students to explain how they found an answer. • Corrects students as needed.	• Includes more than one student in conversation, and purposefully includes students who might otherwise not participate. • Attends to the meaning of the problem (35 total shirts, 16 are red, how many are blue). • Focuses on developing appropriate use of place value language. • Allows students to ask questions to each other. • Encourages students to explain how and why for their solutions.
STUDENTS	• Share their computation strategies. • Share correct and incorrect strategies. • Talk to the teacher.	• Share their computation strategies. • Share correct and incorrect strategies. • Explain the connection between strategies and the meaning of the problem. • Ask each other questions. • Talk to the teacher and to their classmates. • Use appropriate place value language.

The two scenarios presented portray math classroom discourses that have several features in common, such as many students explaining their math work. The purposefulness of the two teachers in organizing the conversation, however, is very different. The teacher in Scenario 1-2 is more focused on

- supporting students in making meaning,
- promoting connections within procedures,
- engaging more students in the conversation, and
- refraining from talking after every student turn.

If the teacher's goal is to develop mathematical understanding for all students in the classroom, Scenario 1-2 represents a more inclusive and supportive type of discourse for instruction.

DEFINING MATH DISCOURSE

In *Principles to Actions* (National Council of Teachers of Mathematics, 2014), the facilitation of meaningful math discourse is listed as one of the key practices for effective teaching and learning. Discourse in math is defined as including "purposeful exchange of ideas through classroom discussion, as well as through other forms of verbal, visual, and written communication" (p. 29). Students have opportunities to express ideas, clarify meaning, construct arguments, and compare approaches to build shared understanding of math concepts as well as flexibility with procedures.

In our work, we think of math discourse as *patterned ways of using questioning, explaining, listening, and different modes of communication in the classroom to promote conceptual understanding in math for all learners.*

Math discourse: patterned ways of using questioning, explaining, listening, and different modes of communication in the classroom to promote conceptual understanding in math for all learners

Because each part of the math discourse definition is important, we like to break it down. Let's start with *patterned*. Classroom discourse is not about the way teachers do something one day or for a few cool lessons. Discourse is created out of the overall structures teachers put in place every day, sometimes without saying anything. Students learn how to participate from what teachers emphasize is valuable. This is why teachers' purposefulness in setting norms for discourse matters. Over time, classrooms develop expected and shared patterns for discourse that become stable. This pattern of engagement during classroom interactions is what we are calling classroom discourse.

THINK ABOUT IT

Think about the proposed definition for math discourse.

What are existing conversation patterns in your math classroom? What do these patterns mean to you when it comes to helping your students learn mathematics?

The second part of the definition is *using questioning, explaining, listening, and different modes of communication*. This clarifies that discourse is made of the questions asked, the explanations accepted, the ways in which teachers and students are listening to each other, and the types of language and nonverbal tools used to present and represent ideas. For example, in Scenario 1-1 the teacher accepts it when Student 1 says that the solution is 35 minus 16 and goes on to say, "I cannot take 6 away from 5, so I cross out the 3 to make 15." In Scenario 1-2, the teacher requires the student to explain *why* subtraction would work to solve the problem and also interrupts some answers to encourage clear and appropriate use of place value terminology. These teachers are listening to and accepting different types of answers from students. Over time, students internalize these messages from their teachers, including what are good questions, good explanations, and useful representations.

The next important part in this definition is *conceptual understanding*. This means that students are learning more than how to carry out procedures with accuracy; they understand the math behind those procedures. Of course we want all students to learn procedures and develop fluency with them. But procedural fluency builds from conceptual understanding and requires efficiency and flexibility. Like in literacy, if a student can sound out a word but cannot comprehend its meaning or use it appropriately, the student is not yet reading. A good example of lack of conceptual understanding comes from an old national assessment item (Carpenter, Lindquist, Matthews, & Silver, 1983) adapted here to use easier numbers. The question asked, "An army bus holds 35 soldiers. If 400 soldiers are being bused to their training site, how many buses are needed?" Many students answered that 11 or "11 remainder 15" buses were needed, which demonstrates procedural solutions. A student with conceptual understanding of division and remainders can find the solution of 11 remainder 15 and knows that 12 buses are needed to seat all 400 soldiers.

The final part of our definition is *for all learners*. All means each and every one. Teachers are responsible for the learning of every child in the classroom, and discourse has to take all of them into consideration. Over time, there cannot be students in the classroom who are consistently excluded from participating. Remember the patterns? Students can participate in different ways on different days, respecting their own identities and areas of expertise. But having students who are seldom engaged or who are rarely asked to answer high-level math questions is a problem! So attention to the patterns of accepted engagement expected from, and actually taught to and learned by, each and every student is key for understanding and activating math talk in the classroom.

DIFFERENT TYPES OF MATH DISCOURSE

Because there can be several different patterned ways of using questioning, explaining, listening, and modes of communication in the classroom, we contend that teachers can use different types of math discourse in the classroom. These types can be used at different times and for different purposes. Figure 1-2 describes four types of discourse that are commonly seen in math classrooms.

Each cell of the Math Discourse Matrix contains indicators of what teachers (T) and students (S) are doing during a particular type of classroom discourse.

Figure I-2 • Math Discourse Matrix

Discourse Dimensions

Discourse Types	Modes of Communication	Listening	Explaining	Questioning
Correcting Discourse	1. T and Ss communicate in T-S-T patterns 2. T favors the use of verbal or pictorial modes when T/Ss share procedures and answers 3. T provides Ss with representations they need to use to solve a problem 4. T favors Ss' use of academic language as "correct"; first or everyday language, if permitted, lacks math connections	1. T listens for correct answers to problems and proper vocabulary 2. Ss listen for T's verification of their answers	1. T demonstrates procedures used to solve a problem 2. Ss present their answers when T asks 3. T praises correct answers and corrects Ss' incorrect answers	1. T asks frequent, short-response questions that attend to Ss' accuracy and speed 2. T asks follow-up questions when needed to lead to correct answers 3. Ss ask T questions to establish correctness of answers
Eliciting Discourse	1. T and Ss communicate in T-S-T-S patterns 2. T makes verbal, pictorial, or written modes available as Ss communicate the answer and how they got it 3. T accepts all representations as equally effective 4. T allows Ss' use of academic, first, and everyday languages equally as modes to share answers and methods	1. T listens for Ss' answers and how they found them, with attention to Ss' vocabulary 2. Ss listen for T's reactions to ensure they have an acceptable procedure	1. T adds to Ss' presentations of their solution methods for solving a problem 2. Ss present their answers and how they found them when T asks 3. T accepts incorrect and less sophisticated answers as indication of Ss' current understanding	1. T asks open-ended questions that encourage many Ss to share their answers and how they found them, expanding the breadth of who participates 2. T asks follow-up questions to support the sharing and collection of several solutions 3. Ss ask T "what" and "how" questions to clarify solution methods
Probing Discourse	1. T and Ss communicate in T-S-T-S or T-S1-S2-S3 patterns 2. T encourages use of multiple modes as Ss share an answer, how they got it, and why they used their approach 3. T encourages Ss' use of various representations to convey math thinking 4. T encourages Ss' use of academic, first, and everyday languages when appropriate to convey math meaning	1. T listens for Ss' explanation of their answer and rationale, with attention to Ss' vocabulary 2. Ss listen to others' explanations to consider if their ideas are similar	1. T revoices and extends Ss' presentations of various solution methods for solving a problem 2. Ss present their answers, how they found them, and why they approached a problem as they did when T or other Ss probe 3. T probes Ss' thinking about incorrect answers to deepen discussion about why they are incorrect	1. T asks probing questions that require Ss to justify their answer, how they found it, and connections between math ideas and representations 2. T asks follow-up questions to press for mathematical depth 3. Ss ask T "how" and "why" questions to clarify their own math thinking
Responsive Discourse	1. T and Ss communicate with significant S-S patterns 2. T requires use of multiple modes of communication as Ss share the answer, how they got it, why, and math connections 3. T expects comparisons across representations to develop math understanding 4. T expects use of academic, first, and everyday languages to develop math understanding	1. T listens for partial and complete understanding in Ss' explanations and connections, with attention to Ss' vocabulary 2. Ss listen to others' explanations to make connections across math ideas	1. Ss restate, extend, and make connections across various solution methods presented 2. Ss volunteer their answers, how they found them, why they approached a problem as they did, and connections to other ideas 3. T and Ss examine incorrect answers so that all Ss can learn from mistakes and connect them to correct solutions	1. T includes pressing questions that promote Ss sharing their answers, how, and why, and connections between math ideas and representations 2. T asks follow-up questions to check that all students are making sense of and connecting math ideas 3. Ss ask one another "how" and "why" questions, taking responsibility for understanding others' math thinking

Discourse Types

Difference in Breadth

Difference in Depth

Difference in Responsibility

Source: Project AII Included in Mathematics, North Carolina State University and Horizon Research, Inc. Copyright 2020. Used with permission.

When engaging their students in these different types, teachers have different goals. For example:

- Correcting discourse can be appropriate for practicing facts.
- Eliciting discourse can support many students in joining the conversation.
- Probing and responsive discourse can develop conceptual understanding and build procedural fluency from this understanding.
- Responsive discourse can support students in taking responsibility for their learning.

We will take a more careful look at each of these discourse types.

Correcting Discourse

Correcting Discourse: a type of discourse that follows the pattern of teacher asks, students respond (what), and teacher verifies the correctness of the answer. It can support speed and accuracy with facts and procedures.

This type of classroom discourse is organized around the teacher initiate–student respond–teacher evaluate (IRE) pattern of discourse in which the teacher asks questions, a student responds (*what* they did or found), and the teacher listens to verify whether the answer is right or wrong. The teacher then moves to accept the answer as correct, or corrects the student and provides the answer, or asks a new question or a different student for the correct answer. For teachers who may have learned math through engagement with this type of discourse, it can become a default pattern to which they turn. This type of discourse can be effective to *access and assess students' accuracy and speed* regarding factual math knowledge and supports recall of facts and procedures. Correcting discourse lacks attention to students' own strategies and does not explicitly promote student engagement with strategic competency, math concepts, or higher-order thinking.

Eliciting Discourse

Eliciting Discourse: a type of discourse in which the teacher elicits and welcomes participation from a broad group of students who share their solutions (*what* and *how*). It can support engagement in math discourse.

The transition between correcting and eliciting classroom discourse involves a *difference in breadth* of what is discussed and by whom. This type of discourse can include a change in turn-taking patterns and wait time so that more students participate in the classroom discourse community, expanding the breadth of who is included in the conversation and what is discussed. The teacher collects several answers to a problem, and students present their mathematical solutions together with explanations of their procedures (*what* and *how*). In this type of discourse, the teacher asks open-ended questions and creates a safe space for students' mathematical thinking. Students feel comfortable knowing that all answers are welcomed and mistakes become nonshameful events. Equally valuing all students' solutions can sometimes mean that less sophisticated mathematical answers, and sometimes even incorrect answers, remain unchallenged and more sophisticated and conceptually rich answers remain unexplored.

Probing Discourse

The transition between eliciting and probing classroom discourse involves a *difference in depth* of the mathematical conversation. Here the teacher transitions from eliciting a collection of student answers to probing students' mathematical thinking and showing appreciation for their mathematical justifications and strategic competence (*what, how,* and *why*). While staying positive and supporting a high level of student participation, the teacher uses questioning to probe for student explanations about their ideas or solutions, including why they were thinking or working in particular ways and what their ideas or solutions mean. The teacher requires students to construct and present their mathematical arguments, with justification. The teacher also encourages students to critique their peers' reasoning while positioning incorrect or partially correct ideas as learning opportunities on which to build. There is a change in what is accepted as mathematical justification and what it means to be engaged in doing math.

> **Probing Discourse:** a type of discourse in which the teacher uses questions to probe students' answers and press for depth in students' explanations of their mathematical thinking (*what, how,* and *why*). It can support understanding and fluency with mathematical ideas.

Responsive Discourse

The transition between probing and responsive classroom discourse involves a *difference in responsibility* within the classroom organization. The teacher moves from being the sole authority for the quality of the content and the nature of the discourse to helping students take responsibility for them. The teacher purposefully works on releasing responsibility for the discourse to students. In turn, students understand that, together with the teacher, they are in charge of helping each other understand math. Maintaining both the eliciting and the probing nature of the two previous types of discourse, the teacher who engages with responsive discourse poses challenging tasks to students and asks them to not only present their thinking and justifications, but also establish mathematical connections among different solutions (*what, how, why,* and *connections*). The teacher expects *all* students to take initiative and to feel responsible for asking each other probing math questions that make thinking and justification available for discussion.

> **Responsive Discourse:** a type of discourse in which students take responsibility for asking each other questions that probe their answers and press for explanations, establishing connections among different mathematical representations (*what, how, why,* and *connections*). It supports reasoning and strategic thinking.

Students become accustomed to comparing and contrasting their mathematical approaches to solving problems, examining similarities and differences across their solutions, and looking for connections. Through these collective, content-rich, and goal-focused math conversations, responsive discourse supports students' development of rigorous math knowledge, including conceptual understanding, procedural fluency, and strategic competence.

HIGH-QUALITY MATH DISCOURSE

From the definitions of the different types of discourse, we can see that high-quality discourse supports the development of all strands of math proficiency: conceptual understanding, procedural fluency, strategic competence, adaptive reasoning, and productive disposition (National Research Council, 2001). High-quality discourse is purposeful and engages students in taking responsibility for their own learning and for the learning of their peers. Although high-quality discourse can include a combination of all types of discourse for appropriate purposes, to support the development of conceptual understanding, probing and responsive discourse need to become the most common and evident patterns in the classroom.

This book focuses on how to move in this direction. With appropriate classroom structures and techniques, teachers can teach all young learners how to engage in responsive discourse—we have seen it emerge and persist in the classrooms of teachers who have collaborated with us.

NOTES

_____

_____

_____

_____

_____

_____

DISCUSS WITH COLLEAGUES

1   How does your definition of math discourse compare to the definition provided in this chapter? Which of the four parts of the definition (patterned; using questioning, explaining, listening, and different modes of communication; conceptual understanding; for all learners) are easier for you to support in your classroom? Which are more challenging? Why?

2   Think about a math lesson you recently taught. Share what happened in this lesson with your colleagues using the discourse features from the Math Discourse Matrix (Figure 1-2). What evidence from your classroom indicates the types of discourse you and your students engaged with during the lesson?

CONNECT TO YOUR PRACTICE

Pick one discourse dimension (questioning, explaining, listening, or modes of communication) under probing or responsive discourse. Plan and implement a math lesson focused on helping students engage in features of that particular dimension. Think about supports your students will need to engage in those ways. After your lesson, consider:

☐   How well did students engage in those features of the dimension? What was successful and what was challenging for students?

☐   What might you do differently in the future to improve student engagement in that dimension?

Engaging Emergent Multilingual Learners in Discourse

Emergent math communicators: students who are learning how to use academic language to communicate mathematically

When teaching diverse students in elementary grades, particularly when working to activate math talk, it is important to start from the premise that all students are, in some form, emergent math communicators. In elementary grades, all students are learning language, including academic mathematical vocabulary, and how to communicate mathematically as they learn math content. This means that the ideas in this book are applicable to all students. At the same time, you can also build on these ideas to support emergent multilingual learners, that is, those who speak languages other than English as a primary language and who are learning both conversational and academic English. In this chapter, we consider who emergent multilingual learners are and the assets they bring to your math classroom. We discuss how to engage them in high-quality discourse and offer practical tools for building on their strengths.

KNOWING MORE ABOUT EMERGENT MULTILINGUAL LEARNERS

To start working effectively with emergent multilingual learners, it is key to see them as individuals under this large label: Each multilingual learner is unique with regard to their histories, assets, capabilities, prior learning opportunities in math, facility with various languages, home environments, needs, and so on. Understanding each of these students individually is therefore key to including them in math discourse and the classroom community.

It is important to know emergent multilingual learners' backgrounds, such as whether they are newcomers (i.e., recently arrived in the country), immigrants but not newcomers, or children of immigrants who have grown up in this country. Students in these different situations can have quite different assets and needs. For example, newcomers may have immigrated for a variety of reasons or they may belong to refugee families who were forced to leave their home countries. Regardless of where they were born or grew up, children may live in homes or communities where the primary language spoken is not English. For some emergent multilingual learners, community and family experiences may mean that they are strong with conversational English.

Emergent multilingual learners also come from different nations and speak various languages. They have experiences with different cultural communities and vary significantly in socioeconomic levels and educational backgrounds. Some students attended school in other countries and know math quite well. Although it might be challenging for them to express what they know, emergent multilinguals' experiences may have taught them communication strategies on which to build. They may have a lot of experiences in learning several languages, which can support their development of more precise academic language in English. Their listening and questioning skills may be especially refined, offering cultural resources that support learning.

> **THINK ABOUT IT**
>
> What do you know about the emergent multilingual learners in your classroom? What are their stories? What are their strengths and assets?

Teachers need to be aware that ways of doing math may vary among cultures, so emergent multilinguals may use strategies or representations that are unfamiliar to you or other students. For example, whereas American students learn to tally using ⊥⊥⊥ to represent five, some Latinx students may show five as ⊠. Connecting emergent multilinguals' math approaches and representations to the work of the class is beneficial to all students. In the case of tallying, both representations support a focus on five as a friendly number or on skip counting by fives. Thus the introduction of these different cultural tools is a beneficial addition to your math instruction.

Fully embracing the commitment that all students can and have the right to learn powerful math is key to successfully teaching math. Conceptual understanding and the procedural fluency that comes with knowing math are not just for those students who can show it or say it quickly. In truth, flexible knowledge and competent communication about math are not likely to come quickly to many students. Thus, the issue is not whether all students can learn mathematics—we know they can! The question is whether we can change the ways in which math is taught so that all students have supportive opportunities to learn and succeed (National Council of Teachers of Mathematics, 2014).

GUIDING PRINCIPLES FOR EFFECTIVE MATH INSTRUCTION OF EMERGENT MULTILINGUAL LEARNERS

Established principles can be used to engage emergent multilingual learners in high-quality math discourse that enables all students to make sense of problems and persevere in their learning. Driscoll, Heck, and Malzahn (2012) suggested three principles when discussing emergent multilinguals:

1. **Challenge students**: It is important to engage emergent multilingual learners in learning opportunities with challenging math tasks. These tasks require students to go beyond using memorized facts or procedures to solve a problem. Engaging emergent multilinguals with these tasks supports equitable access to opportunities to learn.
2. **Use multiple modes of communication**: Communication that is inviting and inclusive of emergent multilinguals uses many types of representations and communication tools. Using gestures, pictures, diagrams, and concrete objects, as well as multiple languages, gives students access to the math and can make the difference between students understanding a problem or lacking the chance to know what is being asked of them mathematically. Multiple modes of communication draw on students' assets to help them think through a problem and more readily express their thinking and reasoning.
3. **Promote academic language**: It is important to support emergent multilingual learners in developing academic language. This means encouraging their preferred communication approaches (such as code-switching, using analogies, or speaking in their first language first) and also helping them connect their ideas to academic English vocabulary, particularly in math. They are experts in learning language; they are doing it all the time!

The strategies they use can benefit your whole class, supporting academic vocabulary development for all young learners as emergent math communicators.

These three principles are embedded in the Math Discourse Matrix (Figure 1-2), particularly in the components of responsive discourse. For example, under modes of communication, the matrix points out the use of multiple modes, including everyday and academic language. Figure 2-1 details a number of ways these principles can be achieved in the classroom. All these ideas can become reality in the classroom when teachers purposefully and appropriately plan for them!

> **THINK ABOUT IT**
>
> How often do you already use these three guiding principles in your own instruction? What might you do to further improve on them?

Figure 2-1 ◆ Guiding Principles of Effective Mathematics Instruction Involving Emergent Multilingual Learners

GUIDING PRINCIPLES	TEACHER ACTIONS
CHALLENGE STUDENTS	• Scaffold tasks to maintain a high level of cognitive demand while building on students' prior knowledge • Question students to extend their thinking and promote sense-making • Model convincing mathematical arguments, clear explanations, a variety of solution strategies, and the process of making conjectures and generalizations • Prompt students to ask questions, consider different solutions, conjecture, and generalize • Encourage students to share their solutions using justifications, convincing mathematical arguments, and clear explanations
USE MULTIPLE MODES OF COMMUNICATION	• Highlight different ways mathematical ideas are communicated (e.g., diagrams, drawings, gestures, technology, concrete objects, mathematical symbols) • Help students learn to diagram mathematically and promote use of diagrams • Provide students with specific tools to communicate mathematical ideas in multiple ways • Prompt students to represent a concept or solution using one or more modes in addition to language—gestures, writing/drawing, technology, concrete objects, mathematical symbols • Make explicit connections between different ways mathematical ideas are represented/communicated

(continued)

(continued)

GUIDING PRINCIPLES	TEACHER ACTIONS
PROMOTE ACADEMIC LANGUAGE	• Provide students with ample opportunity to communicate (e.g., read, write, speak) about mathematics • Vary student groupings to purposefully promote mathematical discussions (e.g., pairing emergent multilingual learners with non-emergent multilingual learners, including peers who can communicate in the emergent multilingual learners' primary language) • Model mathematical language and clear explanations • Prompt students to use mathematically accurate language • Connect mathematical symbols to mathematical language • Rephrase a student's everyday language with proper mathematical language • Request student clarification of statements

Source: Adapted from Driscoll, Heck, and Malzahn (2012).

AVOIDING THE DEFICIT LANGUAGE TRAP

With these ideas in hand, you can engage emergent multilingual learners in discourse in your elementary classroom. Still, it is important to overcome one common barrier: the deficit language that is often used to describe students with terms such as *low, weak,* or *lacking* in math ability. These labels are detrimental for emergent multilingual learners—or any student for that matter. They imply that students have a fixed "math capacity" or "math potential," when often what students are lacking is simply math vocabulary or opportunities to learn.

A critical step to avoid the deficit language trap is to focus on and describe what students can do and consider what they need to do next to continue learning math from a position of strength. Figure 2-2 provides a couple of examples. Using precise descriptive language to identify where students might need to further their math work can help you avoid using generalized terms that assign fixed math abilities to your students.

Figure 2-2 • Examples of Language to Avoid and to Use When Describing Students' Math Learning

AVOID: Deficit Generalizations	USE: Precise Descriptive Language
My language learners don't know any math because they can't subtract.	These two students still need to make sense of place value and regrouping to be able to use the traditional subtraction algorithm.
Tommy is just low because he really doesn't get fractions and can't do fair sharing.	Regarding fractions, Tommy understands the need to use the complete whole. He still needs to understand what it means for the parts to be equal.
I can't call on Xi in class because speaking English is too difficult for her.	Xi can write her ideas in Chinese and in English, so giving her time to write first will allow her to participate more fully in our discussions.

USING APPROPRIATE SUPPORTS IN YOUR CLASSROOM

Throughout this book, and as we introduce the talk techniques, we focus on emergent multilinguals and emergent math communicators, particularly how to support them to fully engage in responsive discourse. In each technique chapter, we mention specific supports or adaptations that you can use to support their growth in learning to communicate mathematically. Here are some general supports that provide language access and promote students' academic language production.

- **Math vocabulary wall:** A list of math vocabulary with pictures and indicators of what the words mean and translations of the words into other languages students know. New words are typically added to the wall as students learn them, or they emerge in discussions. Words typically remain on the math vocabulary wall so they are accessible to students and the teacher throughout the unit, the quarter, or the whole year.

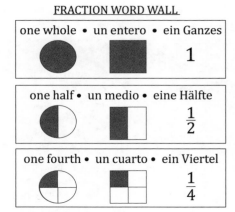

FRACTION WORD WALL

- **Math word bank:** A list of relevant vocabulary students may refer to when it is helpful for sharing their mathematical thinking about a particular idea. The math word bank includes a targeted set of terms related to the content of the day's lesson, purposefully selected and emphasized in discussions to foster development of their meaning as well as students' meaningful use of them.

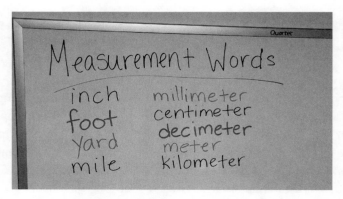

- **Sentence/question starters:** As the name suggests, these are the beginnings of sentences or questions students can use to jump-start their explanations or questions. For example, "I agree/disagree because . . .", "How do you know that . . . ?"

Graphic organizers, manipulatives, and tasks that encourage the use of everyday language and multiple modes of communication are other commonly used supports that allow students to share their mathematical thinking in ways that are comfortable, taking the pressure off of students to use academic language before they are prepared to use it meaningfully. It is important for both emergent multilingual learners and emergent math communicators to understand that their language choices (e.g., first language, everyday language, academic language) and preferred representations are acceptable and encouraged, and can help not just them but the whole class learn more deeply by developing meaning that becomes attached to academic language for everyone.

PROMOTING THE LEARNING OF YOUR EMERGENT MATH COMMUNICATORS

There are a few important ideas to keep in mind as you aim to support your emergent math communicators and multilingual learners in math discourse.

- Get to know them, and focus on the cultural, linguistic, and mathematical assets they bring to the classroom. Doing so respects their unique backgrounds and strengths.
- Explicitly consider emergent multilinguals during lesson planning. Think ahead of time about expectations for their full participation, what assets you can encourage them to use, and what you will do to support them.
- Analyze the tasks you choose, making sure the language and context of problems do not create barriers for your students engaging with and understanding the math. If the context is unfamiliar or requires specific knowledge, provide background, analogies, and visual examples, and invite your students to do the same.
- Model the discourse practices you want to encourage. Demonstrating expectations for how to participate in both math explorations and productive discussions is key!
- Use small-group structures as a "safe space" where it may be more comfortable for emergent multilinguals to communicate their mathematical ideas initially and develop their math communication precision over time. Be purposeful about how you group students, varying your grouping strategies. Provide opportunities for emergent multilinguals to both support and learn from their peers, sometimes working with students who can mentor them and sometimes mentoring others.
- Provide ample time for the rehearsal of explanations before whole-group presentations. Notify students ahead of time that they may be asked to share so they can practice what they are going to say or show while still in a small-group or private setting.

Using these ideas, you can more purposefully attend to and observe how your emergent math communicators and emergent multilingual learners are engaging during math lessons.

DISCUSS WITH COLLEAGUES

1   What grouping strategies are typically used in your school to support emergent multilingual learners? What are the challenges and opportunities when using these strategies?

2   How have you engaged emergent multilingual learners in high-quality discourse and challenging math problems to build on their assets and promote their math achievement?

3   Are there examples of deficit language being used in your school? If so, how might you use precise, descriptive language to change the culture in your school?

CONNECT TO YOUR PRACTICE

Identify at least one emergent multilingual learner or emergent math communicator in your classroom. Jot down the cultural, linguistic, and mathematical assets they bring to a math lesson, as well as their needs. Draw on that information to plan appropriate scaffolds to support and challenge them in an upcoming lesson. After the lesson consider:

☐   How did your knowledge of the student support your ability to help them learn powerful math?

NOTES

_____

_____

Math Knowledge for Facilitating Discourse

An important idea to consider when you start engaging students in probing and responsive discourse is that these types of discourse require more sophisticated ways of knowing math. Most people need to know math for themselves so that they are able to address and solve math-related situations. Teachers, however, need to know math in a very different way when they want to engage with their students' mathematical thinking!

MATHEMATICS KNOWLEDGE FOR TEACHING

The unique way in which teachers need to know math is called Mathematics Knowledge for Teaching (MKT; Ball, Thames, & Phelps, 2008). Of course, teachers have to know how to solve problems that require math and know their answer is right, like everyone else. But teachers need more. Teachers need to know other possible solutions that differ from their own, how these solutions are mathematically related, and what makes certain solutions more sophisticated than others from a formal math standpoint. When a student makes a mistake, teachers need to know not only that there is a mistake, but also what might be correct about the students' thinking, where the mistake is, and why the student might have thought their idea was appropriate. Many times, students' mistakes are overgeneralizations of previously learned procedures, and these overgeneralizations have to be addressed to help students understand what parts of their thinking really are correct and what parts they should rethink and why.

> **THINK ABOUT IT**
>
> When teaching for conceptual understanding, what math knowledge do teachers need to have? Why is that? In which ways do you think this knowledge is different from the math knowledge of other professionals?

Let's return to the math problem from the scenarios in Chapter 1 in which students were calculating 35 – 16. Some students said the answer

Teaching rules vs. teaching understanding of math concepts

was 20 because they included the 16 when counting up—and why don't we? And what if a student said that 35 minus 16 is 21? This student might be missing place value knowledge and inappropriately applying a "rule" such as "always take the smallest away from the largest" to each place value separately, so at the ones place, we have 6 − 5 = 1. Thus, 21 might not be a careless mistake. Rather, it is the product of the student's internalized rules for subtraction. Teachers need to figure out what is going on behind students' incorrect or incomplete mathematical thinking. An internalized rule such as "take the smaller away from the larger" (which students learn from the numbers they see in subtraction in the early grades) can create problems later when learning negative numbers. So this is not a productive way to think about subtraction, and it is important for teachers to address it.

There are also situations when students are solving problems correctly but in ways that the teacher may not have considered before. Suppose a student says the answer to 35 − 16 is 19 because 36 − 16 is 20 and we need one less. We know the answer is correct—and for most people, knowing so suffices. Teachers, however, also need to know that this type of thinking (called compensation) is quite productive in some situations and worth exploring. So figuring out the math behind students' thinking requires a lot of knowledge about math that is specific to teaching.

In their work, Ball and colleagues (2008) suggested that MKT includes both subject matter and pedagogical content knowledge. Within subject matter content knowledge, they separated common content knowledge that most people need from the type of specialized content knowledge that teachers need. Thames and Ball (2010) suggested that elementary teachers also use their MKT when choosing problems, deciding on numbers to use in these problems, giving explanations, and using math notations.

CONNECTING MATHEMATICS KNOWLEDGE FOR TEACHING AND DISCOURSE

When a classroom transitions toward more responsive discourse for conceptual development and procedural fluency, more mathematical depth and stronger MKT are needed. This knowledge allows teachers to

- listen to and make sense of students' solutions and mathematical ideas;

- ask meaningful math questions;
- press for justifications, connections, and deeper explanations;
- use appropriate modes of communication; and
- provide meaningful explanations that take into account where students are in their meaning-making processes.

So MKT and discourse go hand-in-hand, and the promotion of responsive discourse requires teachers to know the what, how, and why of mathematical ideas, as well as connections among them. This means that working on discourse goes together with working on MKT.

Let's consider the connection between MKT and discourse types in the Math Discourse Matrix (Figure 1-2). When implementing correcting discourse, the teacher might only be listening for specific solutions with the goal of indicating which one is correct. In eliciting discourse, the teacher accepts different solutions without going into much discussion about them. Now what happens when the classroom transitions to probing and responsive discourse? In these types of discourse, it is necessary to ask questions that take students' thinking into a higher level of mathematical understanding and connection. Teachers who implement such discourse carefully plan for these types of questions. They consider the mathematical representations to use, the structures they want to highlight, and the language precision they expect from their students. These types of discourse are more mathematically demanding and less predictable because, without losing track of the mathematical goal of the lesson, the discussion needs to be anchored in what students bring forward. MKT helps teachers plan for discourse by anticipating what is likely to come up and considering how to react, even if everything isn't perfectly predictable. In these types of discourse, teachers need strong MKT to activate math talk.

USING MATHEMATICS KNOWLEDGE FOR TEACHING TO SELECT TASKS WORTH TALKING ABOUT

A fundamental connection between MKT and discourse happens in the selection of tasks to use in the classroom. Thames and Ball (2010, p. 223) listed "choosing and designing tasks" as one of the most frequent aspects of teaching that require MKT.

THINK ABOUT IT

What would make a math task worth talking about in your classroom? What MKT can help you select these worthwhile tasks?

Consider the following two tasks.

Task 3-1	Task 3-2
Mr. Gayles is building a rectangular school garden with two 5-foot sides and two 7-foot sides. What is the perimeter of the garden?	The perimeter of the rectangular school garden Ms. Guilford is building is 24 feet. What are the possible dimensions of the garden?

Now envision a classroom situation in which students are working with their partners on these tasks. What might their conversation sound like? For Task 3-1, students need to know the definition of *rectangle* and *perimeter* and then be able to calculate. Most likely, the discussion about this task focuses on knowing definitions and the accuracy of the calculation. For Task 3-2, students also need to know the definition of *rectangle* and *perimeter*, but they have to consider all possible dimensions for the garden design—including a square garden. They need to look for the math structure in these possibilities and existing patterns they know, such as factors of 24. The discussion of Task 3-2 focuses not only on definitions, computation, and accuracy, but also on representations to use, ways to organize information, regularities in repeated reasoning, and connections among different mathematical ideas. Thus, Task 3-2 offers more opportunities for probing and responsive discourse.

Tasks like these two can be roughly categorized as either discourse-limiting (Task 3-1) or discourse-promoting (Task 3-2). When selecting a task for a lesson, teachers use their MKT to identify a purpose for the task and consider which category it falls into based on that purpose. Figure 3-1 shows some features of these two task types. For Smith and Stein (1998), tasks that promote discourse are high-cognitive-demand ones and can include both tasks that ask students to carry out and examine procedures with connections as well as tasks like story problems that require understanding of the context, knowledge of both mathematical concepts and procedures, modeling with math, and adaptive thinking to apply this knowledge to novel situations. These tasks are worth talking about!

Figure 3-1 • Does Your Task Promote or Limit Discourse?

DISCOURSE-PROMOTING TASKS	DISCOURSE-LIMITING TASKS
• Require cognitive effort due to the newness or the unpredictable nature of the solution • Require examination of task context that may limit or expand possible solution strategies and solutions • Require access to relevant knowledge and experiences to work through the task • Require examination of the nature of mathematical concepts, processes, and relations • Require complex and nonalgorithmic thinking • Require multiple representations and connections among representations	• Require a focus on the answer with attention to its correctness instead of its processes • Require no explanation or explanation focused solely on definitions and procedure without relevance to context • Require reproducing previously learned facts, rules, or formulae • Require no connection to concepts or meaning that underlie definitions or procedures • Require little cognitive demand beyond use of the procedure called for • Require one specifically called-for representation

Source: Adapted from Smith and Stein (1998).

ATTENDING TO YOUR OWN MATHEMATICS KNOWLEDGE FOR TEACHING

This book focuses on promoting high-quality math discourse; strengthening MKT is not its main goal. But while working on discourse, there are several ways for you to improve your own MKT—and doing so matters.

1. Listen to your students' mathematical ideas, and explore the math in those ideas.
2. When reflecting on a lesson or talking to your colleagues, examine students' unexpected solutions (whether right or wrong) and consider the mathematical underpinnings of your students' thinking.
3. Think about common mistakes that you see, and do not assume students are being careless; rather, ask yourself what (incorrect) math assumptions might be leading students to make those mistakes.

4. Take time to examine different students' solutions that are correct, and compare the mathematical models and ideas across them.

5. Develop your mathematical curiosity and ponder: Might unexpected students' correct approaches always work, or do they work only for this problem?

6. Try to understand your students' approaches so well that you can anticipate possible mistakes or use their specific approaches to solve new problems.

Let's return once again to the problem in the Chapter 1 scenarios that can be modeled with 35 – 16. Consider the idea of solving this problem with compensation by thinking that 36 – 16 = 20 and we need one less, thus the answer is 19. What would it look like to use this same strategy to solve 94 – 29? And how about using the same compensation strategy to solve 424 – 348? Make a habit of posing these types of questions to yourself or your grade-level team once you identify an interesting student solution.

There are, of course, different ways to think about the problems listed in the preceding paragraph, including different compensation strategies. For the sake of not leaving those problems hanging, and using the same compensation strategy described before, here are some ideas to consider (and you may have others).

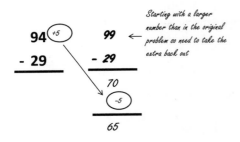

Starting with a larger number than in the original problem so need to take the extra back out

1. 94 – 29 is similar to the 35 – 16 problem because regrouping is needed in the ones place, but it is different in the sense that the difference in the ones place is 5 (between 4 and 9) and not 1 (between 5 and 6). So in this case, you could solve this problem by adding 5 to the 94 and calculating 99 – 29 = 70. Now you compensate by taking 5 away, and the answer to 94 – 29 is 65.

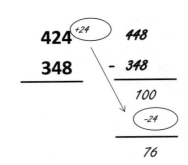

2. In 424 – 348, we need to regroup in both the ones and the tens places. So we could add 24 to 424 and solve 448 – 348 = 100. Now to compensate, we are left with solving the problem 100 – 24. We can do 100 – 20 = 80 and 80 – 4 = 76 if we count backward to avoid regrouping.

These examples are meant to illustrate ways in which you can work on always improving your own MKT by focusing on your students' math work and taking their approaches to a different level of math exploration. The numbers selected for these new explorations were carefully considered to create different situations in which to test a particular mathematical solution strategy. Remember, of course, that there are other ways to solve these problems, including other forms of compensation. For example, you can compensate by adding to the subtrahend instead of the minuend—what do you think happens in this case?

The important idea here is that by analyzing students' mathematical thinking, teachers can create opportunities to discuss their MKT with colleagues in professional learning groups. There is a lot you can learn from students' math and from working with your colleagues. Over time, doing so continues to strengthen your MKT.

DISCUSS WITH COLLEAGUES

1   Think about a recent math lesson you taught where the goal was to develop students' conceptual understanding. What task did you use? Why did you select this task? Use Figure 3-1 to determine if the task was discourse-promoting or discourse-limiting. How did your task features impact students' opportunities to learn the targeted math?

2   What is a recent student math solution that surprised you? Why was it surprising, and what does it mean mathematically? If no students' solutions surprised you, consider: Is it because you already compiled a list of typical solutions and analyzed them or because you are not opening enough spaces for students to surprise you with their mathematical ideas?

3   Do you have examples of math solution strategies that your emergent multilingual learners have shared that are unusual to you but might be commonly used in other communities? Analyze them to understand the math behind them.

CONNECT TO YOUR PRACTICE

Look through your math instructional materials. Are the tasks in the materials worth talking about?

☐ Find a discourse-limiting task and modify it to have more discourse-promoting features. Then use it with your students.

☐ After the lesson, refer to the Math Discourse Matrix (Figure I-2) to reflect on the types of discourse that emerged in your classroom.

NOTES

_____

_____

_____

_____

_____

_____

_____

_____

_____

_____

_____

_____

_____

KEY TAKEAWAYS ABOUT HIGH-QUALITY MATH DISCOURSE

Chapters 1–3 defined high-quality mathematics discourse as well as different discourse types, discussed how to engage your emergent multilingual learners and emergent math communicators in discourse, and also examined what teachers need to know mathematically to promote high-quality discourse in their classroom. Here are the main takeaways from these chapters:

- Different patterns of discourse lead to different discourse types, which can be used for different instructional purposes.

- Spend most of your time in probing or responsive discourse when the goal of the math lesson is to develop students' conceptual understanding and procedural fluency.

- Recognize your emergent multilingual learners as different individuals, and know their stories, strengths, and assets.

- Engage your emergent multilingual learners by challenging them, using multiple modes of communication, and promoting academic language.

- Strong MKT helps you guide your classroom toward more responsive discourse for developing conceptual understanding and procedural fluency.

- Use your MKT to select discourse-promoting tasks that showcase your students' thinking, and mathematically analyze your students' work to continue to strengthen your MKT.

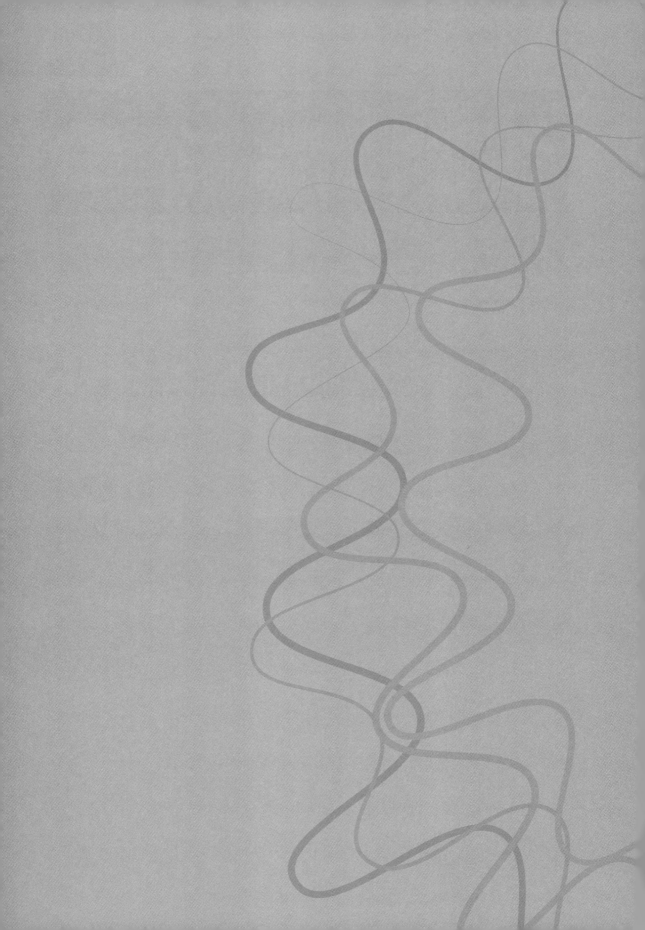

Activating Math Discourse in the Classroom

So you have articulated a vision for how you'd like math discourse to happen in your classroom, you're committed to engaging all students in productive math discourse, and you have a firm understanding of how your Mathematics Knowledge for Teaching will help you promote it. But the question remains: How do you make it happen?

To help you get started, Part II addresses two important pieces that set the foundation for activating math talk in your classroom:

• Establish a math discourse community (Chapter 4).
• Structure your lessons to support high-quality discourse (Chapter 5).

Without a purposefully established discourse community, math discourse can be chaotic. The norms, instructional moves, and practices introduced in Chapter 4 can help you support and foster this community in your classroom. The structure of your math lessons can also provide regular opportunities for productive mathematical discussions to happen. In Chapter 5 you'll learn how to organize your math instruction to activate high-quality discourse.

These steps will get you started—the techniques we introduce in later sections will make you an expert.

Teaching Students to Talk About Math

Math discourse community: a classroom of students who know what is expected in math discourse, how to engage in productive math discourse, and when the discourse is advancing their math knowledge

With the premise that all students can learn—and need to learn—to talk in productive ways in math classrooms, we introduce techniques that teach students how to engage in high-quality math discourse. During math instruction, however, teachers also use a variety of norms, moves, and practices to establish and maintain student participation. This participation creates what we call a math discourse community, that is, a classroom of students who know what is expected in math discourse, how to engage in productive math discourse, and when the discourse is advancing their math knowledge. These norms, moves, and practices have been discussed in the math education literature, and we briefly present them here before adding our techniques to the toolbox of resources teachers can use to activate math talk.

SETTING NORMS

Groups create standard behaviors that become accepted and expected in the ways they interact. These behaviors are called norms. Teachers, intentionally or unintentionally, are constantly setting classroom participation norms. Two types of norms are particularly important in math classrooms: social norms and socio-mathematical norms.

Social Norms

Selecting students who raise their hands before they speak, allowing students to help others, or complimenting collaboration among learners are some of the many ways in which teachers set social norms in their classrooms. Teachers define with their instructions and actions how students are to act during individual work, small-group work, and whole-class discussions; how to start the day and how to leave the classroom when the day is over; and how and when to use classroom resources. We call these routines social norms because they represent the ways in which students are expected to engage with the teacher, their peers, the content, their environment, and existing resources. These norms become the expectations for students' participation, and students are quick to pick up on them—and they also pick up on which norms are only stated versus the norms that are, in fact, expected day in and day out.

In classrooms where responsive discourse is happening, the social norms should be such that students know they are expected to ask questions of each other, explain their thinking, solve problems in a variety of ways, collaborate, respect their peers' ideas, and feel comfortable taking risks and maybe making mistakes—among many others. Teachers are to build trust and develop a learning environment that supports these actions. And for that, the beginning of the year is key. That is the time when the teacher communicates to students what will be expected in terms of classroom behaviors and interactions. That is also when students may test which of the stated expectations will, in fact, become part of the classroom norms.

Social norms are important in every classroom—for example, a classroom in which students are embarrassed to make mistakes allows for little experimentation and discussion of potential misconceptions. However, norms about the math itself are also needed to ensure high-quality discussions.

> **THINK ABOUT IT**
>
> What additional norms that are specific to math might be needed to help promote student participation in responsive discourse?

Socio-mathematical Norms

To address the depth of mathematical discussions, we attend to what researchers have called socio-mathematical norms (Yackel & Cobb, 1996). Let's differentiate between social and socio-mathematical norms by referring once again to Scenarios 1-1 and 1-2 presented in Chapter 1. In both scenarios, students had to explain their thinking— this was a shared social norm between the two classrooms. However, what was accepted as a good mathematical explanation differed in the two classrooms. For example, when asked to explain their answer of 19, Student 1 in Scenario 1-1 proceeded to describe the steps of the subtraction algorithm and that was accepted as the needed mathematical justification. In Scenario 1-2, the teacher first had the student explain why subtraction was an appropriate operation to use for solving this problem, so this student returned to the problem context to start explaining their mathematical argument. These are different socio-mathematical norms. The teacher asking questions is a social norm. Making sure the questions pushed for conceptual explanations and mathematical connections, instead of asking for step-by-step descriptions of executed procedures, is a socio-mathematical norm.

Figure 4-1 provides examples that differentiate social and socio-mathematical norms. It helps you think about when in your classroom you are dealing with norms that define general participation and when you are dealing with norms that are math specific and determine the quality of math interactions. Making sure you are attending to both types of norms helps you make responsive discourse a reality in your classroom.

Figure 4-1 • Social and Socio-mathematical Norms

SOCIAL NORMS	SOCIO-MATHEMATICAL NORMS
Students explain their thinking.	Explanations consist of math arguments that go beyond a procedural summary of steps taken to solve the problem.
Students question each other's thinking.	Students ask each other questions that press for mathematical reasoning, justification, and connections among ideas.
Students collaborate to solve problems.	Collaborative work involves individual and collective accountability for the content; groups negotiate solutions through mathematical argumentation.
Students solve problems using a variety of approaches and they explain their strategies.	Students compare their strategies and results looking for mathematically important similarities and differences. They make connections between mathematical ideas represented in the solution strategies.
Students see making mistakes as a natural part of the learning process.	Mistakes are viewed as opportunities to rethink current conceptions and examine alternative ideas. They support new conceptual learning about math.

Source: Adapted from Kazemi (1998).

USING INSTRUCTIONAL MOVES

Several instructional moves can be used in your classroom as you are working to establish a math discourse community. Chapin, O'Connor, and Anderson (2009) suggested several moves that we have used in our own work to promote responsive discourse. These moves are different from the techniques we present later because they are to be used on a more frequent basis, as part of the routine ways in which the classroom operates. They help teachers scaffold student engagement, enabling all students to participate in classroom discourse. The talk techniques we present in Parts III, IV, and V require further planning and offer more formal participation structures for the students to learn to engage in high-quality discourse.

> ## THINK ABOUT IT
>
> How do instructional moves help all students, particularly emergent multilinguals, engage in features of responsive discourse listed on the Math Discourse Matrix (Figure I-2)?

Figure 4-2 summarizes the instructional moves Chapin and colleagues (2009) proposed, which can be deliberately added to your instructional repertoire: Say More, Add On, Revoice, Restate, Agree or Disagree, and Wait Time. The figure also adds one move we have observed in the classrooms of great teachers: Take Stock.

Figure 4-2 • Instructional Moves

Say More	The teacher encourages students to clarify and share more of their mathematical thinking. The teacher can ask questions such as Can you say more about your answer? Can you expand on what you just said? Tell us more about your thinking. Say More allows students to further explain what they initially said and helps other students gain a better understanding of their mathematical reasoning. Say More can be especially beneficial for emergent multilingual learners: They have opportunities to further explain their own mathematical ideas, and they get to hear their peers further explain their ideas.
Add On	The teacher asks students to engage with and provide more ideas concerning the mathematical reasoning of others. Once a student has shared their mathematical thinking, the teacher can prompt others to Add On to it or pursue it in more depth. For example, if Anthony just presented an idea, the teacher may say to Tamicia, Tamicia, can you explain what Anthony just said and discuss what you think about it? Or when Marcela and DeVonte present different solutions, the teacher can ask, Brianna, we have different solutions to this problem. What do you think about them and what do you want to add to this discussion? Using Add On encourages more students to participate in a discussion, attend to the mathematical arguments of their peers, critique the reasoning of others, and establish mathematical connections among ideas. For emergent multilinguals, it provides an opportunity to connect their ideas to what was already shared, building on ideas that are already available in the math discourse community.
Revoice	The teacher repeats what a student said, often providing some small reorganization or using important math vocabulary. Typically, after Revoicing, the teacher asks the student whether the interpretation is correct. For example, when Li says that $\frac{1}{2}$ and $\frac{2}{4}$ are the same, the teacher can Revoice: Li is saying that $\frac{1}{2}$ and $\frac{2}{4}$ are equivalent fractions. Right, Li? Revoicing supports all emergent math communicators by calling attention to and making sure students can hear important mathematical ideas with precise vocabulary. It also helps verify and clarify the teacher's interpretation of a student's response and can be used when other students may be confused by their peer's response. When this is the case, the teacher can repeat or slightly rephrase a student's mathematical idea, making it available to classmates and giving them another opportunity to hear it.

(continued)

(continued)

Restate	Similar to Revoice, Restate verifies and clarifies an interpretation of a student's response. However, Restating is done by the students. Typically, a teacher asks another student to Restate what a classmate said and then follows up to check whether the interpretation was correct. The teacher can say, Ahmed, can you say again what John just shared? Or Mariana, can you explain in your own words the solution strategy that Drako presented? Sometimes students Restate an idea using slightly different language, making it available to classmates and giving them another opportunity to hear it. For emergent multilinguals it is helpful both to be asked to Restate an idea already shared and to listen to peers Restating their ideas. Restating promotes active listening as well as in-the-moment opportunities for informal assessment of students' understanding of others' mathematical arguments.
Agree or Disagree	Asking students to Agree or Disagree with their peers (like a quick thumbs up or down) engages students with the mathematical reasoning of others. Once a student has shared their mathematical thinking, the teacher can invite others to either agree or disagree with this thinking and explain why. Making sure students understand the ideas with which they are being asked to agree or disagree is key. And asking students to justify their position is also very important. Thus the Agree or Disagree move is typically followed by a "why" question. When using Agree or Disagree, students can hear multiple solution strategies or explanations (valid and invalid) and are encouraged to apply their thinking to someone else's ideas and make connections, which supports all emergent math communicators. Using this move requires a culture in which disagreeing with ideas is accepted and encouraged to promote healthy discussions.
Wait Time	Wait Time gives students an opportunity to carefully formulate and organize their mathematical thinking and reasoning before sharing it with the rest of the class. It encourages participation and gives students the space and time necessary to respond thoughtfully. Typically, teachers know to wait at least 5 seconds before calling on a student to answer a question. However, Wait Time can also be used after that student has been called on so the student can further prepare the response. It can also be used after a student answers a question to allow students to react, ask each other questions, or discuss ideas among themselves—all actions that are part of responsive discourse. Wait Time communicates a message to students that they are all expected to participate, rather than relying on the same few eager ones. Although the silence can be uncomfortable, Wait Time increases the number of students participating in the discourse, encourages communication among students, and supports engagement of emergent math communicators or multilinguals.
Take Stock	Take Stock highlights mathematical ideas that have surfaced in a discussion and helps students make sense of and draw on those ideas in further discussion. This move is typically implemented during small-group time or a whole-class discussion, when the teacher stops the conversation to provide or ask for an overview of important ideas that are circulating in the discourse community. Take Stock helps to organize or focus the mathematical discussion around targeted ideas for the lesson. These ideas may have come up in several groups, or they may have been presented to the class at different times or by different students, and stopping to take stock can bring them to everyone's attention. For example, in a geometry discussion about quadrilaterals, the teacher can stop the class and say, In all the groups, I am hearing this question about whether a square is a rectangle. This is important. Before we move on, what conclusion have you reached? Take Stock gives the teacher an opportunity to help students make mathematical connections among ideas, or address some misinterpretations or misconceptions that can be derailing the work, and then move forward.

Adapted from Chapin, O'Connor, and Anderson (2009).

IMPLEMENTING PRACTICES FOR ORCHESTRATING DISCUSSIONS

Together with norms and moves, teachers use a set of practices for orchestrating mathematical discussions (M. S. Smith & Stein, 2018). Different than moves, which often engage students in doing something during discussions, these practices represent what the teacher is doing "behind the scenes" to make sure the discussion is progressing in a productive fashion. Smith and Stein (2018) explain that these practices allow teachers to be in control of lessons that are designed to unfold around student mathematical thinking. Further, these practices avoid the pitfall of the teacher asking, "Who wants to share?" and then not being able to bring the class discussion back to its goals. The practices are Anticipating, Monitoring, Selecting, Sequencing, and Connecting and are explained in Figure 4-3.

Figure 4–3 ◆ Five Practices for Orchestrating Discourse

Anticipating	Anticipating happens prior to enacting a math lesson. The teacher solves every math problem and creates a list of possible strategies students might use. Anticipating what students might do allows the teacher to preselect some ideas to be discussed in the classroom so that the teacher is not purely improvising during a discussion. By Anticipating, the teacher designs a tentative plan for how the discussion will unfold and decides on how solutions and mistakes that typically emerge can be discussed. Anticipating is a foundational practice that supports all others.
Monitoring	Monitoring occurs during the lesson. It happens when the teacher is interacting with the students, discussing their individual or group work, examining their solutions, and pushing their mathematical thinking. While Monitoring individual or group work, the teacher is also noticing students' actual solutions available for discussion and checking whether and in which ways anticipated solutions and mistakes are emerging.
Selecting	Knowing what students are doing and having the discussion in mind, the teacher Selects which solutions need to be shared with the whole class. Many of these solutions may have been anticipated. Some may highlight assets of emergent multilinguals. Some may include incorrect ideas to be discussed if the classroom is a safe space where mistakes are valuable learning opportunities. When Selecting ideas to be shared, the teacher can let the students know they will be asked to share. In this way, students can prepare for sharing by further organizing their ideas or even rehearsing what they will present. For emergent multilingual learners, this advance notice can allow for more productive participation.

(continued)

(continued)

Sequencing	Once solutions are selected for sharing, the teacher purposefully decides the order in which these ideas will be presented based on the goal of the lesson. For example, if the teacher's goal is to build toward a more formal procedure, shared solutions can build from less to more mathematically sophisticated or efficient approaches. Or the teacher can group presentations by mathematical strategies (e.g., all additive strategies and then all multiplicative ones) for comparisons across strategies. If the classroom environment allows for mistakes to be shared productively, the teacher may start with a correct solution followed by an incorrect solution as a means to compare the thinking involved or to address common mistakes conceptually.
Connecting	As students share ideas in a sequenced fashion, the teacher is facilitating the Connecting of these ideas with one another and toward the goal of the lesson. Students present their arguments and critique others' reasoning. They interact with each other's ideas to engage in responsive discourse. The teacher asks questions and encourages students to ask questions of their peers. The teacher's guidance makes sure the questions and responses address needed focus and depth so that the discussion promotes conceptual understanding of the mathematical ideas at hand.

Adapted from M. S. Smith and Stein (2018).

Let's use Scenario 1-2 from Chapter 1 again as an example that highlights these practices in action. In that classroom, second graders used several different ways to solve 35 – 16: traditional subtraction algorithm, counting up by tens and ones, counting up by ones, and counting backward (that the teacher decided not to pursue). There was also a mistake to be addressed about whether the 16 should be included when counting up. Knowing these solutions were available among students (through Anticipating and Monitoring), the discussion could have gone in several ways depending on how the teacher Selected and Sequenced the different solutions. For example:

1. **Building toward the formal algorithm:** The discussion can start with counting up by ones, address the mistake about counting the 16, go to counting up by tens, then perhaps include counting backward by tens (if available), and conclude with the more traditional algorithm. Connecting across these solutions can help students create meaning for the steps of the more formal procedure. This sequencing of the discussion, going toward the more formal algorithm, can be appropriate if the goal is to highlight the subtraction algorithm as an efficient approach and examine it, with connection to the meaning of the operation, as the culmination of the lesson.

2. **Highlighting the value of counting strategies:** The discussion could omit the traditional algorithm to focus on counting strategies, perhaps encouraging students to add new counting strategies after the selected ones are shared. This discussion builds toward efficiency with mental math and the value of grouping numbers or making tens. It can also highlight ideas about place value in the number system.

Through the practices of Anticipating, Monitoring, Selecting, Sequencing, and Connecting, you can be sure to guide productive math discourse in your classroom while honoring students' ideas. What matters is the goal for the lesson, the knowledge of what solution strategies are available among students, and the purposeful selecting and sequencing of these solutions to guide the discussion toward the goal. The five practices offer teachers an organization for mathematical discussions that are productive in building toward the goals of the lesson. They focus on what the teacher is doing and can be used alongside the talk techniques we introduce, which focus on what the students need to do to learn how to engage in high-quality discourse.

TAKING STOCK

Like the great teachers we have observed, we want to stop and Take Stock of the many ideas presented in this chapter before moving forward. We have discussed the creation of a math discourse community. We suggested teachers need to establish both social and socio-mathematical norms in their classroom for the community to engage in more probing and responsive discourse. We presented several moves teachers can use to help students engage with math (Say More, Add On, Revoice, Restate, Agree or Disagree, Wait Time, and Take Stock) as well as practices that help teachers take control of how mathematical discussions unfold (Anticipating, Monitoring, Selecting, Sequencing, Connecting). Together, these tools help you get started in building toward high-quality discourse. The talk techniques this book adds to the mix are about teaching students how to engage productively with the dimensions of discourse presented in the Math Discourse Matrix (Figure 1-2): questioning, explaining, listening, and modes of communication.

CONSIDERING LITERACY TECHNIQUES

THINK ABOUT IT

What techniques do you currently use in literacy to help students engage in productive conversations about what they are reading and develop their comprehension skills? How could you adapt these techniques for math instruction?

In our work, we have found that techniques are important to explicitly teach students how to talk productively in math lessons. Working closely with colleagues who are experts in elementary literacy, we considered the techniques they were using to promote discourse in literacy instruction and asked: How can we use these techniques in math lessons? The work of adapting techniques from literacy and then adding them to the list of what teachers can do to improve math discourse is the core of this book.

In literacy education, techniques are used to promote discourse that fosters comprehension. These techniques are designed to support students in making meaning of text or in communicating their ideas with clarity and precision. In math, making meaning of text and communicating ideas with clarity and precision are also important features of productive discourse. Particularly in the elementary grades, when one teacher is typically working with students on several subject areas, these techniques can be learned and implemented across disciplines to create a single classroom communication culture (remember the patterns and the norms?) that values productive conversation among students. Talk supports learning in all subjects.

Many people still have this idea of math lessons as a space in which students work quietly on practice exercises. Although we support the idea that there is time for such quiet practice and correcting discourse in math, math lessons should, in general, be like strong lessons in other subject areas: a lively communication arena where students are making sense of the world around them. We suggest that you consider all the subject matter areas in which you teach and ask:

- Where am I being most successful as a teacher in activating high-quality discourse?
- What am I doing in those lessons that is working well, and how can I use similar ideas in other subject matter areas or when I am teaching different content to my students?

These were exactly the questions we asked our colleagues in order to start designing math talk techniques. But before we get to those, let's examine the overall organization of a math lesson to allow for these techniques to be successfully implemented.

DISCUSS WITH COLLEAGUES

1   Think about discussions that happen in your literacy and your math lessons. What are the norms that guide these discussions? Are they similar for literacy and for math?

2   Which of the instructional moves do you use to promote high-quality discourse in your classroom? What has been successful about implementing these moves? What has been challenging?

3   Where in the Math Discourse Matrix (Figure 1-2) do you see features of teachers using aspects of the five practices: Anticipating, Monitoring, Selecting, Sequencing, or Connecting?

CONNECT TO YOUR PRACTICE

Choose a math problem from a lesson in your current instructional materials and anticipate the different strategies your students may use to solve the problem. As you plan that lesson, determine how to sequence these solution strategies in a way that best elicits the key mathematical ideas.

☐   Why did you choose this sequence?

☐   How did it play out in the lesson?

NOTES

_____

_____

_____

Chapter 5

Structuring Math Lessons for High-Quality Discourse

Planning a successful math lesson is much like planning a road trip. First, you need to decide on your destination or end goal. What is it that you want your students to understand at the conclusion of the lesson, and how do you want them engaged in both the math and the discussions in order to make that happen? Second, with that goal in mind, you need to carefully plan out the best route to get there; anticipate the potential roadblocks; and consider the appropriate materials, instructional strategies, and supports needed to successfully arrive at that final destination. Over time, you create a structure for your trips that you find works with your students. You learn the best time to get started, when you need to stop, how far you can go, and what to do when something does not go as planned. This overall structure becomes your travel guide.

> ## THINK ABOUT IT
>
> Before reading further, think about the current structure of your math lessons.
>
> How are your math lessons typically organized? In what ways is this organization different based on the goal of your lesson? How do you plan for this road trip?

In our work with teachers, we use a general navigation tool to help purposefully plan for math lessons and carefully consider what needs to occur when the goal is for students to engage in responsive discourse for conceptual learning. We call this tool the Math Teaching Guide for Responsive Discourse (Figure 5-1). Reflective of a general math lesson structure (Hiebert, Morris, & Glass, 2003; Van de Walle, Karp, & Bay-Williams, 2018), the guide is organized around five phases: pre-lesson Plan; lesson enactment of Launch, Explore, Discuss; and post-lesson Reflect. Each phase contains specific instructional objectives that attend to the math learning and high-quality discourse intended at that point. In this chapter we discuss each of these phases to help teachers design and navigate math lessons that promote responsive discourse.

The Math Teaching Guide starts with planning the lesson. The teacher then enacts the lesson by launching the planned activities, having

Figure 5-1 • Math Teaching Guide for Responsive Discourse

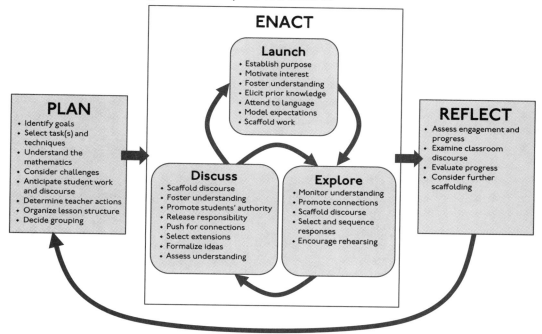

Source: Project All Included in Mathematics, North Carolina State University and Horizon Research, Inc. Copyright 2020. Used with permission.

students explore and solve problems, and engaging them in a whole-class discussion that connects ideas and solutions to build toward and reach the goal of the lesson. This enactment cycle of Launch, Explore, Discuss can happen once or several times within a lesson, as students progress from one problem to the next or engage with different parts of the same problem. After the lesson, the teacher reflects on what happened during the lesson. You can think about the Launch, Explore, and Discuss phases as the "inner" ones happening during the enactment of the lesson and visible to students. The Plan and Reflect phases are the "outer" ones in the sense that they happen apart from enactment of the lesson and are invisible to students.

Before diving into each phase, we reiterate that this lesson structure is meant for promoting responsive discourse. It might be different from lesson structures you are currently using or have used in the past for other instructional goals. However, when the goal is to promote conceptual understanding and build procedural fluency, it is important to open spaces for students to challenge themselves, solve novel problems, construct and share their mathematical argumentation, explore the affordances of different solution paths, and discuss their ideas and strategies.

Although the phases of the lesson follow the chronological order of Plan, Launch, Explore, Discuss, Reflect, to look more closely at these phases we will start with the important goal of having a productive mathematical discussion in the enactment. Then we will work backward. This means we start with the Discuss phase to consider what needs to happen at that point, and then we address what needs to happen in the Explore and Launch phases to make sure the discussion is productive. Only at the end do we consider what needs to happen when you plan for and reflect on your math lesson.

THE DISCUSS PHASE

Discuss Phase: phase of the lesson when the teacher facilitates a whole-group discussion of the math work students have done to foster connections among and sense-making of key mathematical ideas

The Discuss phase of lesson enactment is when the teacher facilitates a whole-group discussion of the math work (i.e., solutions proposed for the math task) with the goal of fostering sense-making of key mathematical ideas. In many ways, this is the culmination of the activity, the moment when students get to share their mathematical solutions and arguments, examine the reasoning of others, connect mathematical ideas, and summarize their work in ways that support their math learning. The Discuss phase needs to be well organized and carefully orchestrated to build toward the math and discourse goals of the lesson. Considering who will share, for what purpose, and in what sequence is a big part of the teacher's role in preparing for the Discuss phase. Then the teacher actively orchestrates the discussion, engaging students with the math and with each other, asking questions, and supporting students as they ask and answer each other's questions. The teacher makes sure students have opportunities to connect mathematical ideas and representations, and are building toward the goals of the lesson.

Purposes of the Discuss Phase

- **Scaffold** whole-group engagement in responsive **discourse**
- **Foster** students' **understanding** of one another's thinking
- **Promote students' authority** to justify mathematical ideas
- **Release responsibility** to students for responsive discourse
- **Push for connections** among ideas and representations
- **Select extensions** for re-exploration of ideas
- **Formalize** students' understanding of key **ideas**
- **Assess** student **understanding** of the math

During the Discuss phase, it is important to engage all students, including emergent multilingual learners, in active participation. Whether students are explaining their mathematical thinking and justifying their solutions, listening to others' explanations, asking each other questions, or identifying connections among ideas and representations, they are all responsible for making sense of the math and formalizing their understanding.

> ## THINK ABOUT IT
>
> Given the teacher's goals for the Discuss phase, what needs to happen prior to this phase to get students to the point at which they can have productive discussions?

THE EXPLORE PHASE

Let's take a look at the Explore phase to get a better sense of the work both the teacher and students need to do as a setup to the Discuss phase. The Explore phase of lesson enactment is when the teacher facilitates students' engagement in the math task. For many reasons, Explore is a critical part of the lesson; it is when students are working intensively on the math, making sense of and persevering in solving problems. When organized using student pairs or small-group settings, the Explore phase is a time when all students have opportunities to productively engage in the math and contribute to extended discussions with smaller groups of their peers. Thus, the Explore phase is often when the most student-to-student discourse occurs. Students collaborate on the task, construct their mathematical arguments, explain their thinking to each other, provide justifications, actively listen to one another's mathematical reasoning, and ask each other relevant math questions to clarify or challenge their thinking. The teacher is mainly monitoring and scaffolding students' work during the Explore phase; this phase is primarily about students' investigation of the math tasks.

Explore Phase: phase of the lesson when the teacher facilitates students' engagement in solving the task and with all dimensions of responsive discourse using individual, pair, and small-group work

Although the Explore phase is often organized as small-group work, it is important to remember the value of giving individual students private think time. Students, including emergent multilingual learners, need structured opportunities to gather and organize their own thoughts before sharing with their peers or having their peers either influence or potentially short-circuit their thinking. Making private think time a regular routine at the start of pair or small-group work holds students more accountable to the math work and leads to more equitable engagement. Private think time also supports emergent multilingual learners in drawing on their assets as they organize their ideas and prepare ways of communicating them.

private think time

It goes without saying that a productive Explore phase does not automatically happen. Students, especially in the early elementary grades, do not yet know how to engage in the ways described above. They need to be taught. They need guidance. They need multiple opportunities and structures within which to practice these skills. For teachers, the Explore phase is a time to actively scaffold and develop these skills with their students. It is also an opportunity to get the lay of the land and make deliberate decisions about how to facilitate the whole-group discussion to come.

Purposes of the Explore Phase

- **Monitor** mathematical understanding through listening and asking questions
- **Promote** mathematical **connections** and use of representations
- **Scaffold** engagement in responsive **discourse**
- **Select and sequence responses** for sharing and discussion
- **Encourage rehearsing** in preparation for sharing and discussion of mathematical ideas

Depending on the nature of the work and the goals of the lesson, executing the Explore phase can be somewhat challenging. However, this phase can also provide incredible insights and rewards for both you and your students. The question is: How can teachers get the most out of the math explorations and small-group discussions? One key is in the Launch.

THE LAUNCH PHASE

Launch Phase: phase of the lesson when the teacher engages students in making sense of the math task, making sure students have access to the math, understand what they need to do, and are ready to get started

The Launch is the phase of the lesson enactment when teachers prepare students to engage in the selected math task and responsive discourse. A well-launched lesson can run quite smoothly because students understand what they need to do and how to get started. On the other hand, when the Launch does not achieve its goal, the teacher can spend quite a bit of instructional time going around and re-explaining the task to students or to groups and helping students get going. The problem with this later situation is that students are sitting idle, waiting for the teacher to come by to even start working—a less than desirable situation.

Finding the balance in which the Launch is not too short that students are not ready or too long that it takes up most of the lesson or does most of the work is a challenge. Thus, thinking carefully about the Launch can help you implement it effectively. Here are some questions to think about when working on launching the lesson and students' work on a particular task:

> **THINK ABOUT IT**
>
> Think about the most recent math lesson you taught. How did you start that lesson, and why did you start it that way? How did the start of your lesson influence the rest of it in terms of student engagement and learning?

1. What do students need to know and understand to be able to get started on the problem?
2. How much information needs to be revealed during the Launch without lowering the cognitive demand of the task at hand?

Purposes of the Launch Phase

- **Establish purpose** for the task(s)
- **Motivate interest** and need to know
- **Foster understanding** of the task(s)
- **Elicit** and assess **prior knowledge** of math and needed vocabulary
- **Attend to language** and representations needed to support students' work
- **Model expectations** for the work and discourse
- **Scaffold** math **work**

Depending on the specific purpose, the Launch may involve a large amount of teacher talk. That seems contradictory to the goal of promoting discourse in the lesson, right? You want *students* to engage in responsive discourse, but *you* may be doing much of the talking at this point. To clarify, the Launch is the time when you set the stage and provide the necessary guidance so students can do the math work themselves and engage in productive conversations with their peers in the Explore and Discuss phases. You will be talking. You may be modeling. But be careful. The Launch is not meant for telling students how to solve the problem they will be working on. It also is not meant for teaching new content. And it is not meant for you to provide a demonstration of a similar problem that students can then copy when solving the assigned one. Furthermore, as we mentioned, the Launch is *not* meant to last the entire lesson; it is the opening of the lesson, usually lasting about 5–10 minutes.

THE PLAN PHASE

Plan Phase: phase of the lesson when the teacher identifies math and discourse goals, selects appropriate tasks and techniques to use, and decides on how the lesson will unfold

The Plan phase, as important as it is, is not one that students get to witness! This is when the teacher identifies goals, selects tasks and techniques, and decides how the lesson will unfold. When planning a lesson that is meant to promote responsive discourse for conceptual learning, there are a few extra important ideas to consider. First, it is critical to ensure you select discourse-promoting tasks (Figure 3-1). You need to think about the math learning goal, the cognitive demand of the task you will use to achieve your goal, and how to make sure you maintain your lesson at a high level of cognitive demand. Then you want to engage with the practice of anticipating. Solve the task yourself and also think about how your students might solve it. Based on your anticipating, you can also preselect and sequence likely solutions to consider how you can organize the lesson around students' thinking and toward your math goals.

One important feature of planning for responsive discourse is to set discourse goals for your lesson. You might want to engage more of your students in mathematical discussions than in the past. You might choose as a goal to engage your emergent multilingual learners in ways that draw on and highlight particular assets. You can focus on your questioning or on what students are offering as explanations. There are lots of specific discourse goals that you can set for your lessons as you start to work on and then continue to strengthen the quality of the math discourse happening in your classroom.

Purposes of the Plan Phase

- **Identify** math content and discourse **goals** for the lesson
- **Select** the **task(s) and** discourse **techniques** that support the goals of the lesson
- **Understand the math** involved in solving the task(s) and the context of the task(s)
- **Consider challenges** that the context of the task(s) may pose for students
- **Anticipate student work and** the **discourse** they will engage in
- **Determine teacher actions**, such as questions to ask, necessary explanations, what to listen for, and modes of communication
- **Organize** the **lesson structure** for Launch, Explore, and Discuss phases
- **Decide grouping** arrangements and sharing formats

THE REFLECT PHASE

After you have planned, and have enacted the Launch, Explore, and Discuss phases of a lesson, comes the Reflect phase. Reflection is a key mechanism for instructional improvement and something that should not be taken lightly. During the Reflect phase, the teacher considers their students' mathematical understanding and the classroom discourse, aiming to both diagnose where students are with respect to math learning and discourse and make decisions about where the classroom instruction needs to go next.

Reflect Phase: phase of the lesson when the teacher considers students' mathematical understanding and the nature of discourse to take stock of where students are and make decisions about where to go next with instruction

Purposes of the Reflect Phase

- **Assess engagement** with **and progress** toward the math content and discourse goals
- **Examine** the nature of the **classroom discourse** in relation to questioning, explaining, listening, and modes of communication
- **Evaluate progress** toward broader math goals beyond the lesson
- **Consider further** structures for **scaffolding** and support that might have improved the lesson

The Reflect phase is also a time to compare what was anticipated for the lesson during the Plan phase and what actually happened. What mistakes did students make? What new solutions emerged that were not anticipated, and what do these new solutions indicate about students' mathematical understanding? Taking notes during the Reflect phase can help inform your subsequent plans or improve the same lesson for another time. The Reflect phase, therefore, closes the lesson cycle and concludes your road trip!

DISCUSS WITH COLLEAGUES

1   How does the Launch-Explore-Discuss lesson structure compare to lesson structures you already use in your classroom and at your school?

2   What are some of the challenges or barriers teachers might experience when trying to implement the Launch-Explore-Discuss lesson structure in their math classrooms? What might be needed in each phase to make it effective?

3   What might be important discourse goals for your current classroom? In what ways would addressing these goals enhance students' participation? How would they support your emergent multilingual learners?

CONNECT TO YOUR PRACTICE

Choose a high-demand task from your current instructional materials that addresses a math goal for your students. Organize a lesson to develop students' understanding of key mathematical ideas from that task.

☐   Plot out how you would Launch the task to prepare students for the math and discourse throughout the lesson.

☐   Write out steps for how you would organize the classroom for the Explore phase. Be specific about what students need to be doing, how, with whom, and which resources are needed.

☐   Specify what you intend to accomplish in the Discuss phase and how you will engage your emergent multilingual learners, and all students, to reach the goals.

NOTES

_____

_____

_____

KEY TAKEAWAYS ABOUT ACTIVATING HIGH-QUALITY MATH DISCOURSE

Chapters 4 and 5 addressed the importance of establishing a math discourse community that supports and fosters high-quality discourse among your students as well as purposefully planning and structuring your math lessons to promote such engagement and learning. Here are the main takeaways from these chapters:

- Activate a responsive math discourse community, putting in place both social and socio-mathematical norms.

- Use available moves and practices to foster productive math discourse in your classroom.

- Establish discourse goals when planning for your lessons to implement high-quality discourse; attend to these goals alongside your math goals as you enact the lesson; check on these goals again when you reflect on your lesson.

- Connect the phases of the Math Teaching Guide to clear purposes and instructional objectives to promote probing and responsive discourse.

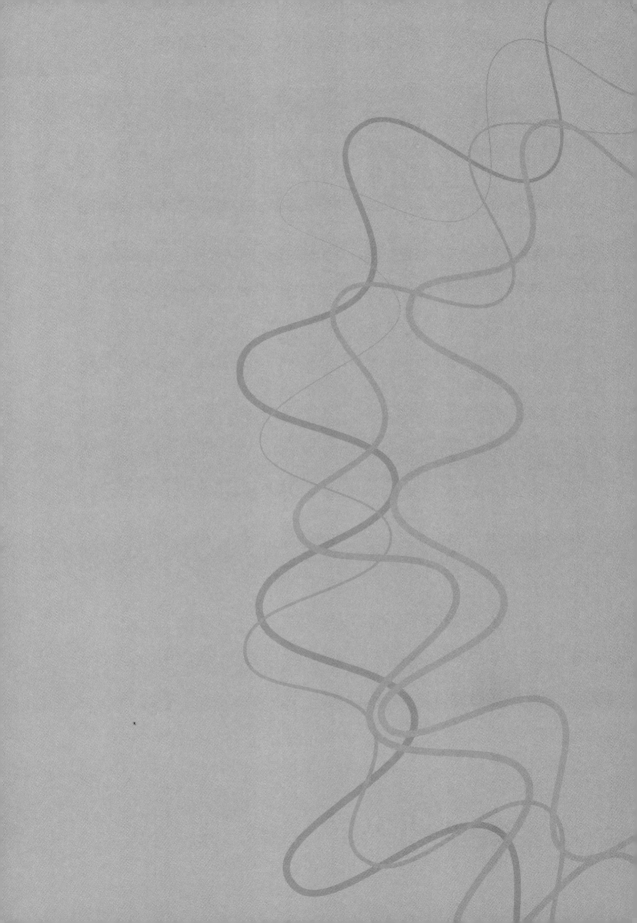

Talk Techniques for the Launch Phase

With the Math Teaching Guide (Figure 5-1) as your general navigation tool to help you purposefully plan your math lessons for conceptual learning, how you launch your road trip plays a critical role in your students' abilities to navigate the terrain and reach the math and discourse goals you've set out for them. Part III of the book focuses on the Launch phase and describes three talk techniques teachers can use for specific purposes:

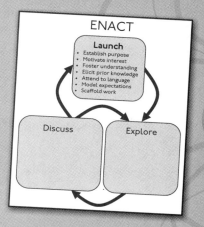

- Story Problem Retelling (Chapter 6)
- Task Think-Aloud (Chapter 7)
- Math Bet Lines (Chapter 8)

The chapters in Part III all use a similar structure to present these talk techniques for the Launch. They also include a vignette from a real classroom to illustrate the talk techniques used for specific purposes. Two points are important about these vignettes. First, teachers taught a complete lesson although the vignettes focus only on the Launch phase. Second, the vignettes are not meant to be exemplars of practice. Rather, they share the experiences of real teachers in real classrooms as they implement Launch talk techniques and reflect on what worked well and what they may do differently next time.

Story Problem Retelling

Connection between math and literacy story telling

Every elementary student solves story problems in math. And every student experiences storytelling in reading and writing. Most students love telling stories! But many students might not recognize that story problems and storytelling are connected. They may not have experienced storytelling *in* math. The Story Problem Retelling technique, derived from the retelling process used in literacy instruction (Mandel Morrow, 1985), is designed to engage students in storytelling that will advance their math learning.

WHAT IS STORY PROBLEM RETELLING?

Story Problem Retelling: a structure that engages students in telling or representing a story problem in their own ways to identify the important elements and actions of a problem before operating on the specific quantities

The Story Problem Retelling technique is a structure that engages students in telling or representing a story problem in their own ways to identify the important elements and actions of a problem before operating on the specific quantities. After reading a story problem to the class, the teacher asks students to retell the problem as a means to assess and foster understanding of the task. Students share their own interpretation of the problem context using multiple modes of communication—their own words, actions, pictures, gestures, objects, or other modes that help them communicate what they understand about the problem, allowing them to take ownership of it.

WHY MIGHT YOU USE STORY PROBLEM RETELLING?

There are a number of reasons for using story problems to teach math. Well-designed story problems can make math motivating for students by showing how math relates to their lives and interests. Story problems can also make math useful by helping students understand the world around them. And story problems can make math accessible and meaningful by giving students insight into how they can identify and represent key parts of math problems, choose ways to solve those problems, and make sense of the math in their solutions within the story situations.

But you've probably seen students in your classroom take numbers from a story problem, choose operations to perform on those numbers, and give the result as the answer. Often the operations they choose seem out of line with the story, and their result does not always answer the question. You might think what they are doing does not make sense, but it must make sense to them. So you might describe what they are doing as using math that does not match the story. But does that mean they don't understand the math or they don't understand the story? Perhaps it is really both, because they need to learn to understand the story *mathematically*. Here's where using Story Problem Retelling in the Launch phase of your lessons can significantly help your students because that is exactly its goal.

Story Problem Retelling offers a way for students to do the important math work themselves when they are faced with a challenging problem. Like other stories, the math stories in problems often have multiple parts that fit together in a sequence or connect in some other way (e.g., a beginning, middle, end). Story Problem Retelling can help students account for and represent the different parts of the math story to help them identify what kind of solution will complete the story.

Comprehension of math problems is at the heart of Story Problem Retelling. Reading and listening are normally associated with comprehension, but this technique engages students in explaining and using various modes of communication, both dimensions of the Math Discourse Matrix (Figure 1-2), to improve their comprehension. As an example, second-grade students might read or listen to this problem:

> Millie's Diner had 94 clean plates for serving sandwiches and 58 clean bowls for serving soup. After a busy day serving lunch, there were just 27 plates and 12 bowls still clean. How many sandwiches and how many bowls of soup were served for lunch?

Students probably could not repeat this problem verbatim. They probably could not keep all of the numbers in their heads either. Those are not the goals of Story Problem Retelling. Rather, with this problem, the technique should engage students in recognizing and communicating that there are both plates and bowls, plates are used to serve sandwiches and bowls are used for soup, and some are still clean. If students can wrap their heads around that much of the problem before working with the numbers, they are demonstrating good comprehension because the known and unknown quantities will match specific parts of the story as they understand it. And if they use pictures or objects to show the plates and bowls, they are well on their way to representing and solving this problem.

Purposes of Story Problem Retelling

- Support access to and comprehension of the task students will be solving
- Help students articulate what they think the task is asking them to do
- Develop common language for students to use as they work on the task
- Spark initial ideas for solving the task

Accomplishing these purposes during the Launch phase offers students a good start for everything that comes later in the Explore and Discuss phases, including working with their peers to solve the task, justifying why they chose a particular solution strategy, explaining their use of the selected strategy, presenting their mathematical argumentation, and making mathematical connections.

GETTING STARTED WITH STORY PROBLEM RETELLING

To implement the Story Problem Retelling technique, use the following steps:

1. Read the selected story problem aloud as a class, or read it to the class if your students aren't ready to read aloud. For more complex problems, you might read it aloud two or three times.

2. Tell students that before they solve the problem, it is important to really understand the story, especially the math parts. Encourage them to think:

- *What is the context of the problem? What is happening?*
- *What do the numbers in the problem mean?*
- *How are the numbers related to each other?*
- *What are the actions in the problem?*
- *How are the actions related to the numbers in the problem?*

3. Give students brief quiet time to think about how they will retell the story themselves. They may want to read the problem silently again or write down their ideas.

4. Call on a student to retell the story in their own way. Their story should describe the important mathematical elements and actions of the problem, without worrying about the specific numbers. Explain that they can use words, drawings, actions, and objects to tell the story.

5. If students are simply rereading the story problem again or are getting too focused on the specific numbers, you may want to stop showing the problem or have students put it aside and try again.

6. Ask a question or invite a question before moving on, which can clarify or emphasize what has been shared.

7. Call on another one or two students who may have a different way of retelling the story, and allow questions again.

It is vital that any serious misunderstandings about the story be resolved right away. Some students' retellings may introduce incorrect information or an incorrect interpretation. Use students' questioning or your own to ensure each retelling is ultimately accurate. These conversations are important because they can really help all students with the work of comprehending and successfully solving a story problem.

SIGNS OF SUCCESS

- Students focus on the important mathematical elements, actions, and relationships in the story.

- Students meaningfully use academic and everyday language, or other modes of communication, to retell the story accurately.

- Students' retelling suggests ways for them to represent and solve the problem.

CAUTION SIGNALS

- Students focus only on the numbers and getting them right when they retell, not attending to the actions and relationships in the story. (Suggest that they retell the story first without using the specific numbers so they can describe actions and relationships.)

- Students retell about the context but overlook the elements, actions, and relationships that matter mathematically. (Use prompts or questions that point to the important mathematical parts of the story.)

SUPPORTS THAT HELP WITH STORY PROBLEM RETELLING

Story Problem Retelling in math has some unique features that you probably would not find when using this technique in another subject area. When retelling in a math lesson, students should be focused on the situation and action of the story in terms of mathematical meanings. Their retelling should communicate understandings of what the quantities (both known and unknown) in the story mean; what actions in the story (putting together, comparing, grouping, etc.) point to mathematical operations; and what the task is asking them to do (sometimes answering a question, but sometimes coming up with an explanation, a justification, or some other mathematical response).

Sentence starters. To help students get started with their retelling and have it focus on the math, you may consider using sentence starters like "This story problem is about . . . ," "The numbers in this story tell us . . . ," or "This problem is asking us to . . . ." You may also want to tailor some sentence starters to the actual problem, such as "On a busy day at Millie's Diner . . . ."

Math word banks. Math word banks can suggest ideas and language for students to use as they retell the mathematical components of the story. After you read the story problem, and before students retell it, your class can brainstorm useful words that you record for everyone to see.

Varied language. As students retell, they will choose a variety of words to share their understanding, and those words might mix academic mathematical language with everyday language. Both are valuable and should be encouraged. Allow students to practice using some academic mathematical language they see as relevant and use everyday language to interpret or communicate something that perhaps isn't so familiar in academic language. Remember, it isn't just the person who is retelling that benefits; everyone listening has another opportunity to understand the math story.

Guiding questions. It will be helpful to prepare question prompts ahead of time so you can guide students' retelling toward the essential information. To come up with these questions, think about what your students are likely to leave out in their retelling.

 Sharing responsibility with students. When used in the Launch phase, Story Problem Retelling typically involves just a few students who retell the problem to the whole class. To broaden student participation as well as encourage active listening and student-to-student communication, you can invite other students to ask the reteller questions for clarification or use moves like Restate, Agree/Disagree, or Add On to their retelling. Doing so gives the students more responsibility and ownership of the conversation.

> ## THINK ABOUT IT
>
> As a support, what sentence starters would help your students retell the Millie's Diner problem? What important aspects of the story problem would you want to make sure are present in the Story Problem Retelling?

IMPROVING AND ADAPTING STORY PROBLEM RETELLING

Depending on your purpose for using Story Problem Retelling, the implementation of it may vary. Some adaptations for this technique are listed below, but you will probably come up with others once you and your students are comfortable with this technique.

Focus on the question. Let's say you want to use this technique to help students analyze a story problem to determine the mathematically important and unimportant information for answering a specific question. Deciding what information is important and how to use it are skills students must develop to become powerful mathematical thinkers and problem solvers. Toward this goal, you might ask students to retell just the parts of a story problem they would need to solve it.

Try a different kind of problem. Although it is most natural to use this technique with story problems, you also might try it with problems that aren't written as stories but can be understood using stories. The problem may describe a situation that students analyze in order to provide an answer supported with mathematical evidence. For example, you could present students with a graph and ask them to retell the story of what is represented in the graph, such as this fifth-grade task:

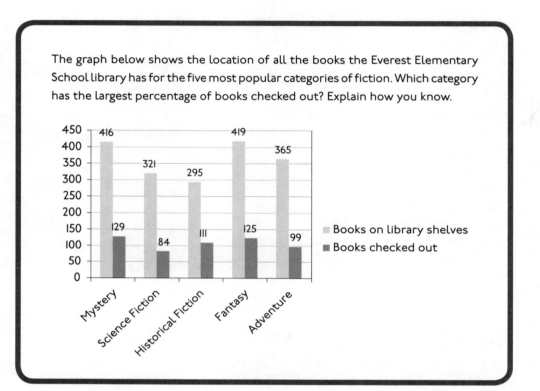

The graph below shows the location of all the books the Everest Elementary School library has for the five most popular categories of fiction. Which category has the largest percentage of books checked out? Explain how you know.

Using the same steps to get started with Story Problem Retelling, you could ask students to retell about the situation and quantities that are represented in this graph, that is, a story about students checking out books from a school library. In this case, the students would be engaging with the problem in a way that gives them access to the math story and ownership to solve the problem and make sense of their answer.

Make mistakes acceptable. Because Story Problem Retelling is not just recalling and repeating, but making sense of a problem, it is important to know that not everything your students say will be correct. Developing a classroom environment where it is okay to make mistakes and work through them is essential for students to develop conceptual understanding of challenging ideas. Story Problem Retelling in the Launch phase of a math lesson can be a way to address students' initial confusion and mistakes, recognizing them as part of the problem-solving process. It can also invite diverse understandings of the problem and approaches for solving it so your class can work together to develop every student's understanding. Planning carefully with clear purposes for using Story Problem Retelling in a lesson and anticipating what students might say or do will help you achieve your instructional purposes and support your students' best learning.

EXAMINE PRACTICE

Read the following vignette from Ms. Ladeaux's classroom, where Story Problem Retelling is used two times during the Launch phase of a lesson. What purposes might Ms. Ladeaux have for each use of the technique?

Story Problem Retelling in Ms. Ladeaux's Kindergarten Classroom

Planning the Lesson

After 13 years teaching first grade, I am in my first year teaching Kindergarten. My story shares my experience launching a lesson on addition and subtraction within 10 using Story Problem Retelling. My class had been exploring the idea that adding or subtracting 1 gives the next, or the prior, number on the counting sequence. We also worked with adding or subtracting 2. So in this lesson I wanted to build on that learning as we worked with bigger numbers within 10. My math goal was for students to realize there are many strategies they can use to solve addition or subtraction problems within 10.

My discourse goals related to the listening and explaining dimensions of the Matrix. I wanted my students to be active listeners whether I was talking, their partner was talking, or someone was sharing with the whole class. I also wanted students to explain their mathematical thinking throughout the lesson. During the Launch phase, I wanted my students to realize they have to listen carefully to the story to know what it is saying mathematically.

(continued)

EXAMINE PRACTICE (continued)

I selected two result-unknown story problems for this lesson: one that required students to add 3 + 7 and one that was 4 + 3. I wanted the class to work on the problems one at a time, doing two rounds of Launch-Explore-Discuss in the lesson. I had planned that, if it went well, we would work on a change-unknown problem as a whole class at the end, during the Discuss phase, and use Story Problem Retelling together one more time. The problem structure was 3 + ___ = 7. We would have just discussed a problem that was about 4 + 3 = 7, so I thought it could go well.

Enacting the Lesson

At the start of the lesson, my 16 students gathered on the carpet. I asked them to share what tools they had been using to solve problems. They talked about using white boards, number lines, ten frames, and story mats. I displayed the first story problem on the board.

> There were 3 bees buzzing in the hive.
>
> Then 7 more bees joined them.
>
> How many bees are in the hive now?

"Put your listening ears on," I said before reading the problem to the class the first time. And before reading it a second time I said, "Close your eyes and visualize the problem." I next asked if someone could retell the story to the class. Jamil volunteered. As he spoke, he drew three bees in the nest on the board and then he gestured when he said, "Seven more are flying in." Before Jamil said the solution to the problem, which I thought he might, I said "Thank you" and kept the focus on the story, not the answer.

Next, Afra volunteered and told the story using her hands. "First there are three bees," she said, showing three fingers. "Then there are more bees that join them," and she just waved her hand. She concluded by saying, "All the bees are together now," and cupped her hands together like the hive, "and we need to find how many that is." I was pleased with both students' Story Problem Retelling because they used visual modes of communication—drawings and gestures, which I knew would help all of my emergent math communicators, including those students with identified learning needs.

> There were 4 bugs sitting on a vine.
>
> Then 3 more bugs joined them.
>
> How many bugs are on the vine now?

Later in the lesson, when I displayed the second problem and read it aloud to the students, I wanted to encourage different students to retell it, so I used some scaffolding questions to support their thinking about what the numbers and actions in the story meant. I said, "We have some different numbers in this story. What do those different numbers mean? What does the action in this story tell us about those numbers?" Then I gave the students one minute to individually think about how they would retell the story themselves before I picked Mikayla and Zhu to retell the story to the whole class. After that, I also had the students turn to a partner and retell this story to one another. They worked in these pairs to solve the two problems in each Explore phase of the lesson. We also got to the third problem I wanted to examine with them during the final Discuss phase.

Reflecting on the Launch Phase

I was very pleased with how the lesson unfolded. I had intended for the students to understand what each of the problems was about, and using Story Problem Retelling was quite useful in accomplishing that goal. The students really did understand the problems before trying to solve them. I thought it was especially helpful that the technique engaged all the students in listening to each other's retelling of the story problem and explaining their own, including the many different kinds of drawings and gestures they used. This kind of experience built my students' confidence with the problems and helped them develop comfort in taking risks in

(continued)

EXAMINE PRACTICE (continued)

our classroom. Some students who are just learning to explain their own thinking did really well retelling the story problems, so that was a big step forward for them. Using Story Problem Retelling made the work on the initial two problems so accessible to all students that we did get to work on the more challenging change-unknown problem as a whole group at the end. I was impressed with my students' focus on what was happening in the stories.

Examining Ms. Ladeaux's Launch Phase

Using Story Problem Retelling in both whole-group and partner work, Ms. Ladeaux supported access to the story problems and allowed all students to make sense of and communicate their meaning for the mathematical elements, actions, and relationships in the stories. In doing so, she helped spark their ideas about how to solve the problem. The Launch phase scaffolded successful math work as students knew what they needed to do in the Explore phase.

DISCUSS WITH COLLEAGUES

1   What modes of communication are familiar to your students for storytelling in literacy or other subjects? How could you use those for Story Problem Retelling in math?

2   What are some misunderstandings you've seen when students solve story problems? How could Story Problem Retelling help students make sense of story problems to avoid these misunderstandings?

3   If a student expresses a misunderstanding when retelling a story problem, what classroom norms have you developed that can make that a productive moment for the whole class?

Connect to Your Practice

Choose a story problem that you can Launch with the Story Problem Retelling technique. As you plan for the lesson:

☐ Identify the sentence starters, some words for a math word bank, and guiding questions that can support your students in retelling this story problem.

☐ Consider other supports that would help your students—materials for drawing, manipulatives, smart technologies. Be creative!

NOTES

Chapter

7

Task Think-Aloud

There are times in reading when students cannot answer questions about what they've read because they didn't understand it. In these cases, providing students with a model for how to go about making sense of text can help them do it on their own. A Think-Aloud is a metacognitive process in which one first reflects on their thinking about what they read and then articulates their thinking to others. When used by teachers, it can help students develop text comprehension (e.g., Davey, 1983; McEwan, 2007; L. A. Smith, 2006). Teachers verbalize their thoughts while reading aloud a difficult passage, articulating their cognitive actions with the goal of supporting students' implementation of similar actions. In math, students also need to make sense of tasks and other information. How can Think-Alouds help?

WHAT IS A TASK THINK-ALOUD?

Task Think-Aloud: an activity in which the teacher models metacognition by reflecting on their own thinking while making sense of a math task, articulating their thoughts aloud for students

Making sense of a math task requires careful consideration of task context or the text of the problem posed. To support this sense-making, teachers can use a Task Think-Aloud in which they share their reflection on their thinking about a math task, modeling and articulating their thoughts for students. So just as the name suggests, the Task Think-Aloud technique allows the teacher to share with the class their metacognitive process regarding their comprehension of the task and what it asks them to do.

Unlike most of the other talk techniques, the Task Think-Aloud is not intended to involve students in a mathematical discussion—quite the contrary. The responsibility for carrying out the Task Think-Aloud

[handwritten notes: "does not involve students" and "Teacher Think aloud"]

68

rests largely on the shoulders of the teacher, who is doing most of the talking. The students' responsibility is to actively listen as the teacher thinks aloud; remember that listening is one of the four dimensions of the Math Discourse Matrix, so developing this skill with your students is critical. When used in the Launch phase, the Task Think-Aloud can make the difference between students being able to work on a challenging task during the lesson or struggling to even begin.

WHY MIGHT YOU USE A TASK THINK-ALOUD?

Purposes for using the Task Think-Aloud technique in your class involve a desire to model specific metacognitive processes for students, which can vary from determining what is important or irrelevant information to considering actions that are key to the mathematical ideas of the problem.

Purposes of Task Think-Alouds

- Attend to context
- Make sense of unfamiliar vocabulary
- Model how to get started
- Determine important or irrelevant information

The situations that follow provide examples of how to use Task Think-Aloud with your students.

Attend to context. Consider the issue of key words. For years, it was a popular strategy for teaching students how to find a solution to a story problem. Students looked for words such as *more* or *less* to help them determine whether to add or subtract. Unfortunately, key words do not foster comprehension and can, in fact, be misleading when students fail to consider the mathematical context of the problem. Using a Task Think-Aloud, you can model for students how to attend to mathematical meaning in a problem and make sense of the situation. For a question like "How many more cookies does

thinking beyound
key words
to decide how to solve problem.

Meetal have than Stuart?", the following Think-Aloud can help avoid the focus on key words:

SCENARIO 7-1

"So this question is asking how many more cookies Meetal has than Stuart. When I think about that, I think that I need to know how many cookies Meetal has and how many Stuart has. And then what do I need to do? I need to find a way to compare these numbers so I can know who has more cookies and how many more."

Make sense of unfamiliar vocabulary. Sometimes, math problems include a new word that you know will stop many students from attending to the math. In these cases, the Task Think-Aloud is an opportunity to model how to create meaning for the new word so that students can make sense of the task and persevere. In Scenario 7-2, the teacher is thinking aloud about a question from a story problem about a souvenir shop at a football stadium. The problem starts by indicating that the shop sells shirts, hats, balls, and a couple of other products, and finally asks, "How many total items of merchandise does the shop have for sale?"

SCENARIO 7-2

"The question asks about the total number of items of merchandise for sale at the shop. Merchandise is a new word for me, so how can I think about it? The problem talks about shirts and hats for sale in the shop, and the question asks about the total number of items. Let me think about the context, like I do when I am reading and there is a word I don't know. I think about the context and look for clues to make sense of the new word. They ask about total items, and I'm thinking that is about what I can buy in the shop, so all the different things for sale in the store must be the merchandise."

Model how to get started. You can also use Task Think-Aloud to help students consider ideas on how to get started or what to do first when solving a problem. This can be useful when complex problems require an initial organization to model the situation with mathematics. For example, if the problem describes the numbers of animals in a zoo, and there are several different animals, you may indicate that representing these numbers can support the mathematical work of solving the problem, as in Scenario 7-3.

SCENARIO 7-3

"The problem says 7 monkeys, 12 zebras, 4 elephants, and 14 impalas. That is a lot of different animals for me to remember at once, and I have to figure out how many animals there are. . . . I think I'm going to begin by showing the different animals. There are a lot of ways I can show that, and I think showing it should help me better understand the problem and come up with a reasonable solution."

Determine important or irrelevant information. Consider also the situation in which students end up taking any and all numbers they encounter in a story problem and then operating on these numbers, regardless of whether these numbers are important for solving the problem. During a Task Think-Aloud, you can share your methods for determining what information in a story problem is really necessary for solving it, as the teacher in Scenario 7-4 does for a problem related to a plan for healthy diet and exercise.

SCENARIO 7-4

"The question is asking about the percentages of different types of food in this diet, so I am thinking whether I need to consider the information about liquids, like drinking 8 glasses of water, or the information about exercise, like walking 0.5 miles. I need to figure out whether they are important for solving this problem, and if they are not, can I leave them out of my representation and solution?"

No matter what you model, whether it is how to think about words, get started, or consider important information, remember that you are modeling thinking in a metacognitive fashion. The goal of the Task Think-Aloud is to give students options for how they may go about making sense of and solving problems themselves.

THINK ABOUT IT

Think back to a recent time when your students struggled to understand what a story problem was asking. How could a Task Think-Aloud have improved your students' understanding and subsequent mathematical work?

As you can see, there are lots of different reasons for using Task Think-Aloud, all of which help set students up for success during the Explore phase. The Task Think-Aloud technique, however, has one big caveat: You cannot use it to demonstrate how to solve the problem or tell students what to do. When you complete your Task Think-Aloud, students should have just enough information to get started with the task at hand; they should not have it almost or already solved for them. A well-done Task Think-Aloud leaves the important mathematical work for the students to carry out and helps them pay attention to their thinking.

GETTING STARTED WITH TASK THINK-ALOUDS

To implement the Task Think-Aloud technique, use the following steps:

1. Determine your purpose for the Task Think-Aloud. What do you want to model? Depending on your purpose, you may have students continue working on the same problem from your Task Think-Aloud, or you may give them a related but different problem to try on their own.
2. Plan what you want to say during your Task Think-Aloud to ensure you will share thinking that supports your purpose. Pay special attention to where you should stop the Task Think-Aloud so that you don't do the important mathematical work for students.
3. Practice your Task Think-Aloud to make sure you do not lower the cognitive demand of the task.
4. In class, tell your students you will do a Task Think-Aloud so they can hear how you are thinking about the problem. Remind students that their job is to practice listening carefully.

We've included examples of the Task Think-Aloud, but there are many more ways to incorporate this technique into your Launch. In particular, when you want to make sure your Launch helps foster understanding, attend to language, or model expectations, the Task Think-Aloud can be a great technique to use. Note that all of the talking in Scenarios 7-1 to 7-4 is done by the teacher, and remember this is a time for the teacher to share and for students to listen; students will have the opportunity to share later when they work on problems.

SUPPORTS THAT HELP WITH THE TASK THINK-ALOUD

Because teachers are the main actors during the Task Think-Aloud, the supports we offer are primarily for them. However, the first support is beneficial for students.

Overwhelming if the task seems hard but task think aloud provides students with a place to start.

Math word banks and representations. Students, in particular emergent multilingual learners, may benefit from a math word bank that displays words defined during the Task Think-Aloud for the duration of the lesson. Similarly, representations created during the Task Think-Aloud can be made available for students to reference throughout the Explore phase.

Scripts. It may be helpful to write out a script for your Task Think-Aloud, at least the first few times you try the technique, to ensure that you convey your intended message. Consider making notes of the things you want to be sure to say as well as the things you do not want to say; for example, you do not want to tell students exactly what to do and take away their challenge during the Explore phase.

Practice. Practice your Task Think-Aloud in front of a peer, and ask for their feedback. Or video-record yourself and, as you watch the recording, reflect on whether your purpose was clear.

SIGNS OF SUCCESS

- Students know how to think about the problem after the Task Think-Aloud, and they engage with the mathematical work of the problem.

- Students use thought processes modeled during the Task Think-Aloud when making sense of their tasks.

- Students attempt to make meaning of their story problem or task, rather than blindly putting numbers together.

CAUTION SIGNALS

- Students call out answers while you are doing your Task Think-Aloud, rather than listening to your thinking. (Remind students that this is your turn to share and they should focus on listening carefully.)

- You realize you've accidentally taken your Task Think-Aloud too far and solved the problem for students. (Ask students to use another strategy to determine if your answer is correct or incorrect and prove it to their peers.)

IMPROVING AND ADAPTING TASK THINK-ALOUDS

Not only can the Task Think-Aloud help students think about how to go about solving math problems; it can also serve as a model for demonstrating how students can talk about their own mathematical thinking with their peers.

Students thinking aloud. After students have experienced several teacher Task Think-Alouds and begin to understand this idea of thinking about problems and their own thought processes, encourage them to think aloud when they are sharing in their small groups or even in whole-group discussions. You may consider doing a Task Think-Aloud during the Discuss phase before asking for student volunteers to share their own thinking aloud with the class. This approach offers a model closer in time, so students do not have to remember back to the beginning of the lesson.

Modeling other forms of discourse. Task Think-Aloud can also be utilized to model other forms of discourse during a math lesson. For example, you can use the technique to model your thought processes when questioning ("I wasn't sure I understood how Marta solved the problem, because I didn't understand one part of her explanation. So I decided to ask her a question about that specific part."). Similarly, you can use it to model your thinking when responding to a question ("Rumi asked me how I made a ten before I added. His question helped me realize that I should explain that part of my solution more clearly, and maybe even in a different way—like with a picture.")

EXAMINE PRACTICE

While you're reading the following vignette, consider how you might think aloud about the task Ms. Ballard proposed to the students. In particular, in the reflection, Ms. Ballard explains that students did not do exactly what was planned. What changes could be made to the Task Think-Aloud to improve students' mathematical work on the task?

Task Think-Aloud in Ms. Ballard's Third-Grade Classroom

Planning the Lesson

The math goal of my lesson was for students to understand that geometric shapes have attributes that define them. My students had not done much geometry until this lesson, but we started reviewing geometric vocabulary. So I planned to have students compare and contrast shapes based on attributes. I wanted them to get experience using their content vocabulary and recall prior knowledge of shapes. I also wanted them to be confident enough to agree or disagree with their partners and to explain their thought processes, similar to what's in the explaining dimension of the Matrix. I therefore had the discourse goals that all students would take risks sharing their mathematical thinking to their partners and use precise geometric vocabulary.

In the lesson, I planned for my 21 students to rotate through the following three activities in groups of 6 to 8, each working with a partner most of the time:

1   **Math With the Teacher:** small groups worked with me on sorting shapes

2   **Math With a Partner:** students completed a tangram puzzle worksheet

3   **Math by Myself:** students individually read books on shapes

I planned to use the Task Think-Aloud technique for the Launch phase because I wanted all my students to think about how they could get started with the sorting activity they would be doing when working with me. Because of the rotation, I had to be detailed during the Launch, and I wanted to make sure I modeled what I wanted students to be thinking about in the sorting activity.

Enacting the Lesson

I started with a little review of geometric vocabulary and reminded students to refer to the vocabulary cards on the Math Word Wall.

(continued)

EXAMINE PRACTICE (continued)

Math Word Wall

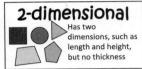

2-dimensional
Has two dimensions, such as length and height, but no thickness

quadrilateral
A four-sided polygon

square
A quadrilateral with four equal-length sides and four right angles

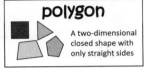

polygon
A two-dimensional closed shape with only straight sides

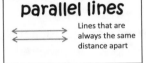

parallel lines
Lines that are always the same distance apart

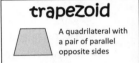

trapezoid
A quadrilateral with a pair of parallel opposite sides

parallelogram
A quadrilateral with two pairs of parallel opposite sides

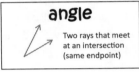

angle
Two rays that meet at an intersection (same endpoint)

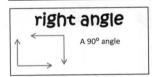

right angle
A 90º angle

I then explained the rotation to be used during the Explore phase and my expectations for each activity. To explain the Math With the Teacher rotation, I used the Task Think-Aloud to model what was to happen in the shape-sorting activity.

I used a set of shapes in the Task Think-Aloud that was different from the set students would be using so students could hear how I was thinking about those shapes but couldn't just copy what I did. On the document camera, I showed them the shapes I had sorted and explained that, at the table with me, I would be giving them some shapes, and they needed to be thinking about how they could sort those shapes in different ways and into different groups. I said that I was showing them one way that I sorted my shapes. "Your sorting will be different," I clarified.

I worked backward and shared with them what I had recorded as the result from my own sorting using an app they are familiar with. I played the recording: "Shapes on the left side have at least one curved edge and some straight edges, but the shapes on the right side only have straight edges. On the right, some are quadrilaterals and some are pentagons, triangles, and other shapes." After playing the recording I said, "Let me share with you my thinking process for how I got to this conclusion. And then, you will be doing your own thinking when you sort your shapes."

I began the Task Think-Aloud by placing the collection of shapes I was sorting on the document camera and saying, "Oh, wow, where do I start? I notice a shape with a curved edge, that catches my attention. And I see there are a few more like that and other shapes with straight edges only. So I can separate them like that—this is sorting." I then demonstrated by separating shapes with curved edges to the left side of the screen and those with all straight edges to the right side (as shown in Figure 7-1). "I noticed that the shapes in my group to the right had all straight edges and the shapes in the group to the left could have straight edges, but not all of them did. So I documented that on my sheet. As I look at the figures again, I am wondering what other groups I can sort them into. I think that is a trapezoid; it has one set of parallel sides and one set of sides that are not parallel. I think I'll look a little more at the other shapes on the right side to classify them as well. They have a different number of sides." At that point students began to chime in, adding that they could see a pentagon or triangles on the right side. This was the end of my Task Think-Aloud.

Figure 7-1 ◆ Shapes With Curved Edges vs. Shapes With Straight Edges Only

(continued)

EXAMINE PRACTICE (continued)

Leonardo, an emergent multilingual learner, looked at a shape on the left with two pairs of parallel sides connected by curved edges. One student was saying this was a rectangle, but Leonardo indicated disagreement. I asked him if that was a rectangle, and he shook his head no, pointing to vertices and indicating these were not right angles (showing a 90° angle with his hands). The other students agreed with his explanation. After this discussion, I explained how I had documented my sorting onto my recording sheet, which is what the students would be doing in the activity. Students then began their rotations.

Reflecting on the Launch Phase

Overall, the lesson went as I thought it would. The slightly longer Launch phase was a bit challenging, but there was a lot to share. Prior to the lesson, I reviewed the Task Think-Aloud technique and put thought into the difference between demonstrating a set of directions versus sharing my mathematical thinking aloud. I think this went well because my modeling led to students being successful during the Explore phase. My students were comfortable taking risks while discussing attributes of shapes with their partners, and I was impressed to hear students using content vocabulary and asking fantastic questions like "What do we call shapes that are not quadrilaterals?" However, a few students were still rather reserved. I hope with more time spent on this topic that they are able to actively participate in richer mathematical discussions with their peers while attending to precision in their language.

At the same time, I also think I did not model the activity as openly as I had wanted. Because I sorted the shapes into curved versus not curved edges first, many students believed that they were expected to start by sorting into those same two categories, which had not been my intention. I had wanted to see a variety of different sorting categories. Still, I think that verbalizing my thought process while manipulating the shapes did give students an idea of how to successfully sort. I was pleased to hear a student explain to another student, "They're categories . . . we're sorting them into categories that we notice." That made my day.

Examining Ms. Ballard's Launch Phase

In this lesson, Ms. Ballard used the Task Think-Aloud technique to model how students could get started on the sorting task. The model proved to be successful in getting students to use categories to separate shapes based on specific attributes so that the students could productively engage with the task, sorting shapes and using math vocabulary meaningfully to describe their work. At the same time, Ms. Ballard's Launch and reflection remind us of the importance of planning carefully for the Task Think-Aloud so students do not think they need to do exactly what the teacher models or, in this problem, start the task exactly in the same way. Always remember: The goal is to model thinking processes!

DISCUSS WITH COLLEAGUES

1   What purposes for Task Think-Aloud might be especially helpful with your students? What would be important to emphasize in a Task Think-Aloud in order to address those purposes?

2   Students' primary participation in the Task Think-Aloud is listening. What can you do to encourage your students' careful, active listening when you use this technique?

3   How would you know if you've taken a Task Think-Aloud too far in the sense that you solved the problem for students? What would you do in that situation? How can you prevent short-circuiting student thinking during the Task Think-Aloud?

CONNECT TO YOUR PRACTICE

Choose a math problem that you can Launch using a Task Think-Aloud.
As you plan, determine your purpose for using the Task Think-Aloud.
Then write a script of what you plan to say. After the lesson, reflect on
how the Task Think-Aloud played out.

NOTES

_____

_____

_____

_____

_____

_____

_____

_____

_____

_____

_____

_____

Math Bet Lines

When learning to read, students are taught not just to decode words and understand each sentence and paragraph, but also to watch for foreshadowing cues about what might be coming in the text, and to use their background knowledge to think ahead and predict what might happen in a story. Students can learn to read math problems in the same way, using their mathematical background knowledge to make sense of what a problem might ask them to do. The Math Bet Lines technique (Dick et al., 2016) is adapted from Bet Lines in literacy instruction. Developed particularly to support emergent multilingual learners, it promotes students' ability to make predictions built on their comprehension of text (Soto-Hinman & Hetzel, 2009). This adaptation for math instruction is geared toward motivating students and helping them apply prior knowledge to make sense of math problems as they read them.

Math Bet lines

Predicting

WHAT ARE MATH BET LINES?

The Math Bet Lines technique uses a simple sentence starter—"I bet . . ."—to prompt students to think ahead as they read a problem to predict what might come next, and ultimately what the problem will ask them to find or do. The teacher reveals only short parts of the problem and asks students to consider what they think might come next. Students can use knowledge of the context for the problem and their prior math knowledge to make appropriate predictions based on their comprehension of the problem. Inviting students to predict parts of the problem supports their motivation to engage with it and their understanding of the situation.

Math Bet Lines: a technique that engages students in predicting the information and question a math problem will include as the teacher reveals the problem one sentence or idea at a time

Scenarios 8-1 and 8-2 offer some examples of the beginnings of problems and bets that students might make:

SCENARIO 8-1

Kindergarten: A problem could begin with *Anya and Lin found 8 rocks.* Students' bets at this point might be "I bet they lost 2 of them," "I bet they already had some other rocks," or "I bet they wanted to share them." The teacher then continues to read the problem.

SCENARIO 8-2

Third grade: A problem could state *Taysha brought a box of 96 chocolates to share with the class on Monday. The class ate 18 of them that day.* Students might predict "I bet it says, 'What fraction is left?,'" "I bet it will say they ate 24 on Tuesday," or "I bet it will ask how many days the chocolate will last if they eat 18 each day."

THINK ABOUT IT

Read Scenarios 8-I and 8-2 again. Which bets give a new quantity? Which ones suggest an operation? Which ones hint at what kind of answer the problem will have?

During Math Bet Lines, you have an opportunity to note how your students read and understand problems, particularly in terms of the ideas they bring to their reading in math. As students make predictions, ask students to reason about the mathematical meaning of each prediction. Does it offer new quantities? Suggest a relationship or action that might indicate an operation? Lead to a question? Hint at what kind of answer they might find? You can also discuss bets that are not mathematical, helping students think about what makes a mathematical contribution, such as if a Kindergarten student in Scenario 8-1 said, "I bet Anya and Lin are friends."

WHY MIGHT YOU USE MATH BET LINES?

To support reasoning, modeling, and problem solving, students should carefully read and comprehend the information and questions that make up math problems. An important skill for reading with understanding is the ability to foresee what might come later in a text

Challenge

based on information the reader takes in. Students find it engaging and motivating to predict new information or a question in a math problem as they make sense of the context, quantities, relationships, or representations included in the problem. Making sense of what they know and considering what else might be coming depends on students connecting to prior knowledge so they can make sensible predictions, home in on strategies for solving, and consider what a solution will look like. The more adept students become at thinking ahead when they read, while also considering what each new piece of information in a math problem indicates, the better they will become at making sense of problems and reasoning mathematically to solve them.

k-1

Math Bet Lines provide a structure that invites all students to communicate ideas and engage with one another's reasoning. Active listening, a key dimension of the Math Discourse Matrix (Figure 1-2), is vital to making this technique work.

Launch

Is it modeling whole group small group

> # Purposes of Math Bet Lines
>
> - Motivate students to read carefully to make sensible predictions
> - Help students tap into prior knowledge about the context of the problem
> - Promote connections to other problems students have seen before
> - Anticipate what additional information or question a problem might include
> - Support students in thinking carefully about what each part of a problem tells them about known and unknown parts as well as operations, approaches, or representations they might use in solving the problem
> - Encourage students to determine, before solving, what kind of answer the solution to a problem will have

Because students do not know for sure where the problem is headed, making bets about what might come next and interpreting the meaning of each bet should be a shared responsibility among the class where every contribution is valued. It is not important who might predict exactly what comes next in a problem, but rather that students learn to make sensible predictions and consider each piece of information in a problem carefully.

GETTING STARTED WITH MATH BET LINES

As part of your planning for using the Math Bet Lines technique, first identify the specific purpose for using it in the Launch of your lesson. Then select the task based on the purpose you identify. Good discourse-promoting tasks for Math Bet Lines involve several sentences or pieces that can be parsed and revealed sequentially, suggesting where the problem might be headed without entirely giving away what will come later. Story problems are typically good choices, but other types of problems that present a situation with data, geometric diagrams, graphs, or the like may also be appropriate. You want to create a sense of anticipation to motivate students to share their ideas.

To implement the Math Bet Lines technique, use the following steps:

1. Ahead of time, break up the problem into sentences or parts that each provide an important piece of mathematical information, but do not give away everything. That is, find places to pause and engage students' thinking as you reveal only part of the problem and invite students' bets.

2. Reveal the first part of the problem and pause for students to consider what might come next. Remind them that their bets should (a) make sense with the information that has been revealed; (b) provide more mathematical information, not just more context; but (c) may or may not be the same as what the problem actually says. That is, appropriate bets are those that make mathematical sense and add useful information.

3. Use wait time to build anticipation and to give all students a chance to think about a prediction.

4. Call on one student to share a prediction using the sentence starter "I bet . . . ." Encourage all students to listen carefully to what the selected student shares. Again, use wait time to give all students a chance to think about what is shared.

5. Engage the whole class in a discussion about the initial bet. First, ask the class if the bet makes sense, and give the student who shared an opportunity to consider this question and respond first. Then invite other students to comment. Second, ask the class to identify what new mathematical information the bet includes—A quantity? A relationship between quantities? An action?

6. Ask if anyone has a different bet to share. Call on another student, and repeat Steps 4 and 5. Ideally you'd like to get

a second bet that would take the problem in a different direction, not just a different quantity with the same action or relationship.

7. Reveal the next part of the problem, and pause again to repeat Steps 3–6 with the new information. Students will likely get excited if one of their bets turns out to be what is included in the problem; you should again remind them that this is not the goal.

As an example, consider the following first-grade problem:

> Rashid and Felicity both started stamp collections. Rashid has 5 stamps to start his collection. Together they have 12 stamps. Does Rashid or Felicity have more stamps to start a collection? How many more?

The Math Bet Lines technique could reveal the following lines to encourage students' predictions:

> Rashid and Felicity both started stamp collections. Rashid has 5 stamps to start his collection.

Pausing here, students can use their prior knowledge of collections to make many possible predictions. A student might say, "I bet Felicity has 10 stamps" or "I bet Felicity gave Rashid some more stamps." Each of these ideas makes sense. The first would add a new quantity. The second would provide information about both a quantity, which is unknown, and an action. Another possibility is information about both collections, which is what this problem actually includes next:

> Together they have 12 stamps.

There are still various ways the problem could go, but students can begin to narrow in on the kind of information likely to come next. The problem could provide more quantities, but it could also ask questions about the information already presented. So students might predict, "I bet they got 5 more stamps." Or they might predict the next line will be "How many stamps does Felicity have?" Both make sense. But students might also say, "I bet it will ask how many stamps did Rashid give Felicity?" The prediction fits the context and is a math question, but it is a question that cannot be answered with the information provided so far in the problem. If a student offers that kind of prediction, it is still important to have a conversation about it so the class can determine whether that is a question that makes sense at this point and why.

To end the Math Bet Lines technique, the last part of the problem is revealed. Students tend to be very motivated to see how the problem ends. This example problem says:

> Does Rashid or Felicity have more stamps to start a collection? How many more?

It is a good idea to have students read the whole problem once it is all revealed. They will have talked about several predictions that would likely take the problem in different directions. That's exactly what should happen! At the end, though, you will want students to focus on what information the problem really provides and what it asks them to do.

SUPPORTS THAT HELP WITH MATH BET LINES

Math Bet Lines is a fairly straightforward technique for the lesson Launch. Many students can engage with it quickly, and students tend to be eager to offer predictions, if not right away, then once they have experienced Math Bet Lines a few times. Additional supports, nonetheless, can help make sure all students participate and provide more structure for whole-class discourse. Here are some supports you can try:

Wait time. Each time you reveal a part of the problem, use wait time to give all students a chance to think of a prediction. And after each prediction, using wait time again is helpful for all students to consider their classmate's bet.

Highlight the key questions. While you are employing wait time, students should be considering two key questions:

1. Does the prediction make sense?
2. What new mathematical information does it offer?

Display these two questions to help students consider them after each bet is offered. Doing so can improve their mathematical reasoning.

Just a few bets. This technique works best when the number of predictions is small, so the class can spend time thinking about each one carefully. You may have different ways to randomly or systematically select students to contribute to discussions; those can be helpful to promote equitable participation in Math Bet Lines. It is important, though, that students do not know who you might call on, so that every student thinks of predictions in case they are selected.

Math word wall. If you have a math word wall or bulletin boards, posters, or other displays, encourage students to use them as sources of ideas and academic language for their predictions. This type of support is especially helpful for emergent math communicators and emergent multilingual learners. If you find that students tend to favor certain kinds of predictions, it can also provide a way for students to think of predictions they might not first imagine.

SIGNS OF SUCCESS

- Students use prior knowledge as an asset to make their predictions.
- Students listen carefully to each other's predictions.
- Students' bets contribute to the mathematical understanding of the problem.
- Students analyze predictions using the two key questions.

CAUTION SIGNALS

- Students make predictions that are unrelated to the problem or only about the context. (Use the "What new mathematical information" question to point out this limitation.)
- Students focus only on guessing what the problem will say, not on what makes an appropriate prediction. (Remind students what makes a prediction mathematically productive.)

IMPROVING AND ADAPTING MATH BET LINES

As you and your students get comfortable with the basics of Math Bet Lines, you can strengthen this technique for your class in several ways.

Turn-and-talk. To support students in coming up with predictions, and to give more students a chance to share a prediction, you can use brief turn-and-talk moments each time you pause for students to generate bets. This support gives all students more practice with math communication, helps students listen to their peers, and offers you the chance to hear some predictions so you can select students you know have different predictions to share.

Return to the key questions. You will likely need to stress again and again that predicting exactly what the problem will say is not the goal. Rather, the goal is to think about what the problem might say that would make sense mathematically. The two key questions for Math Bet Lines (*Does the prediction make sense? What new mathematical information does it offer?*) are essential to using the technique effectively, because they focus on reasoning about the mathematical information presented in a problem. To broaden participation, you might select two students in advance who will ask the class these two questions for each prediction offered. You could choose students who you know always like to speak up to play these roles; that will give other students more opportunity to make predictions. Or you could choose students who tend not to volunteer spontaneously so that they have an active role with this technique and get used to participating. This is a special responsibility, so you will want to rotate which students you choose each time you use Math Bet Lines.

Use with Math Talk Chain. To encourage careful listening, you could combine Math Bet Lines with the Math Talk Chain technique (Chapter 13). In this case, after a student offers a prediction, you can ask other students to explicitly connect what they heard their classmate predict to their response to one of the two key questions, using structures like "I heard you say . . ., which makes sense because . . ." or "Your prediction was . . ., which gave us new information about . . . ."

Review with key questions. Once you have revealed the full problem you use for Math Bet Lines, reviewing it using the two key questions line by line can aid students' comprehension of the math in the problem. In fact, there may be parts that do not add any new mathematical information, or some of the information turns out to be irrelevant for solving the problem. Thoroughly comprehending a problem in this way will help students learn to reason abstractly as they extract key information to model and solve the problem.

EXAMINE PRACTICE

Read the vignette below and ask yourself: When and how could Ms. Tate-Salina have used the two key questions for Math Bet Lines to help students understand the mathematical information in the Lake Glenn and Lake Parker problem?

Math Bet Lines in Ms. Tate-Salina's Fourth-Grade Classroom

Planning the Lesson

My story about using Math Bet Lines with my students shares what happened during a lesson on solving multiplicative comparison problems, which are hard for my fourth graders. My goal for the lesson was for students to conceptually understand the anatomy of this type of problem. I chose to use Math Bet Lines to help them identify the structure of multiplicative comparisons, which will help them tackle more complex problems in the future. I also wanted students to work on questioning; this was my overall discourse goal for the lesson. I wanted students to use Probing and Pressing Math Questions (Chapter 15) when we got to our discussion of these problems. My plan was to model such questions throughout the lesson so students could ask these types of questions of each other later.

This is my fourth year teaching fourth grade, and I have built a resource of favorite lessons. For this lesson, I selected two problems in which the multiplier factor is given. I wanted students to be able to compose the correct equation for each problem. I also wanted them to compare the structures of these problems. My plan was for students to list three things

(continued)

EXAMINE PRACTICE (continued)

they noticed and one thing they wondered about the problems and their structures.

> Lake Glenn in Virginia is 55 miles long.
>
> Lake Glenn is 5 times as long as Lake Parker.
>
> How long is Lake Parker?

> Over the summer, José read 9 books.
>
> Rachel read 4 times as many books.
>
> How many books did Rachel read?

I planned to launch the lesson using Math Bet Lines for the two problems and then have students work in groups to compare them. Using Math Bet Lines would help motivate my students' interest in multiplicative comparison problems. When we started the bets, though, I found out that students needed more time to think about each problem before they could compare the two of them. So I did not get through this lesson as I planned.

Enacting the Lesson

My 25 students gathered on the carpet. I started the Math Bet Lines by displaying "*Lake Glenn in Virginia is 55 miles long*" and asking students for their bets. They know this routine. I gave them a little think time, and then Hasam bet that the other person was about 2 times as big as Glenn—he was thinking about a multiplicative comparison but had misunderstood the context of the problem. Then two other students shared bets that also indicated they thought Glenn was a person. At that point, I wanted to see if a student could clarify this situation, so I asked Lee to share because I could see they seemed surprised by the other bets. "It is not a person. Glenn is a lake," they said. We talked about names of different lakes in our state and quickly clarified this situation. When I asked for more bets, Jonah said, "I bet Lake Glenn is however many times as long as another lake," and Talisha suggested, "I bet the other lake is more." Jonah's bet predicted a multiplicative comparison. Talisha's might lead to a multiplicative comparison, but it could also describe an additive relationship. This was a key distinction to consider in our discussion.

I revealed the next statement: *Lake Glenn is 5 times as long as Lake Parker.* "Think before the hands go up," I said, to give some wait time. During this round, Sidney bet, "How long is Lake Parker?" and I asked why she would think so. Sidney explained this would be similar to an earlier problem in the notebook: "This one says 5 times as many and the other said 6 times as many, so they seem to be similar." I asked if anybody could explain Sidney's thinking, and DeVonte offered, "I think Sidney thinks that because in the other one it says 6 times and in this one it says Lake Glenn is 5 times . . . Sidney thinks they are kind of like the same type of problem." So I revoiced, "What you are suggesting is that the set-ups of the problems are similar, right?" The students confirmed. At this point I showed the last part of the problem: *How long is Lake Parker?* Sidney was kind of excited to be right, but I wanted to make sure we focused on the structure of the problem.

We read the whole problem together. I pushed students to think about the context of the story before solving it: "Before you solve the problem, do you think Lake Parker would be more or less than 55? Create a sketch of your thinking—we are not solving the problem quite yet." I thought this would be a quick extension to my Launch to help students represent the problem visually, and then I would start the Math Bet Lines for the second problem so we could compare them.

When I heard many students saying Lake Parker was more than 55, I noted that the class was divided on their thinking about which lake was longer. I did not think they were ready to compare the two problems as I had originally planned, so I decided to move into the Explore phase for just my first problem and have students work on it. As it turned out, the Math Bet Lines became the Launch for an Explore and Discuss of just this one

(continued)

EXAMINE PRACTICE (continued)

problem, which worked well because many important questions about multiplicative comparisons came up that we were able to address.

Reflecting on the Launch Phase

The Launch phase unfolded as expected, initially, via the Math Bet Lines for the multiplicative comparison story problem. I had anticipated the Launch might get lengthy due to the various potential student questions and misunderstandings, and I would have to do some redirecting. But I quickly learned there was more confusion than I had expected regarding the first problem. I really had to change my lesson, but I was pleased with it because it brought this confusion forward and gave us a chance to resolve it. I was glad to hear students articulate their thoughts and ideas. And they successfully listened to others and respectfully agreed or disagreed with their peers. It was the Launch that made me realize that perhaps my planned lesson was still too ambitious for my students at this point. I was able to reorganize right then and there. I still want to know how seeing the two types of multiplicative comparison problems simultaneously could have contributed to their thinking. This will be for another time. For today's lesson, however, we made progress on students' understanding of multiplicative comparisons.

Examining Ms. Tate-Salina's Launch Phase

This example of Math Bet Lines shows Ms. Tate-Salina using the Launch phase to address two different issues students had with the problem posed. The first was a misunderstanding of the problem context that would have made solving the problem harder. The second was the realization that the prior knowledge needed for this lesson was not in place and the lesson could not proceed as planned. Although the Math Bet Lines allowed for connections to a prior similar problem students had seen, many in the class were not yet making sense of multiplicative comparisons. Realizing this issue in the Launch phase, Ms. Tate-Salina recalibrated and scaffolded the math work for the students based on where they were mathematically at the time of the lesson.

DISCUSS WITH COLLEAGUES

1 How can you support students in making predictions that introduce new mathematical information about quantities and relationships?

2 What can you do to help students decide, and explain their thinking, about whether a prediction makes mathematical sense?

Connect to Your Practice

Choose a math problem that you can Launch using the Math Bet Lines technique. As you plan, identify the places you can break up the problem to pause for predictions and anticipate the kinds of predictions your students might make for each part.

☐ What types of predictions would you like to see?
☐ What types of predictions wouldn't be as helpful?

Once you have planned the problem and its delivery, try Math Bet Lines with your class.

NOTES

_____

_____

_____

_____

KEY TAKEAWAYS ABOUT THE LAUNCH PHASE

Part III presented three talk techniques for the Launch—Story Problem Retelling, Task Think-Aloud, and Math Bet Lines—and their accompanying classroom vignettes. These chapters illustrated teachers attending to different purposes in the Launch to prepare students for productive engagement with math content and in mathematical discussions. Here are the main takeaways from these chapters:

- Use the Launch techniques for specific purposes, and remember that techniques for techniques' sake do not change discourse.

- Set the tone for the work of the lesson with the Launch, and make sure your students can be successful in the subsequent Explore and Discuss phases.

- Do not use the Launch to tell students what to do, and avoid going so far with your Launch that there is little left for students to do or talk about.

- Ensure through the Launch that your students are focusing on the mathematical aspects of the task.

- Use the Launch to gain insights about how students are making sense of the problem, and clarify ideas as needed.

- Calibrate your lesson during the Launch, ensuring that your selected discourse-promoting tasks are appropriate for your students and not too easy or too hard.

Talk Techniques for the Explore Phase

The math lesson has been launched. Students are motivated; they understand the task at hand; they know the expectations and are ready to begin. Now your classroom journeys through the Explore phase in preparation for the big arrival in the Discuss phase.

Part IV of this book focuses on four specific talk techniques you can use during the Explore phase to activate productive student-to-student mathematical conversations and prepare for subsequent whole-group discussions:

- Think-Pair-Rehearse-Share (Chapter 9)
- Math Four Square (Chapter 10)
- Talk Triangle (Chapter 11)
- Solution Draft and Final Copy (Chapter 12)

Similar to chapters in Part III, these four chapters present the talk techniques and include vignettes that illustrate the techniques in action with teachers working in real classrooms. The vignettes for the Explore phase techniques are designed to give you great insights into how students work together when solving discourse-promoting tasks and what teachers are doing as students are working on the math.

Think-Pair-Rehearse-Share

In literacy, strategies like Readers Theatre (Young & Rasinski, 2009) give students opportunities to practice reading and rereading a script that they may later perform for the class, building their confidence as readers. Just as actors need to rehearse their lines before presenting to a large audience, students need opportunities to prepare and rehearse their mathematical explanations before sharing with the whole class. The Think-Pair-Rehearse-Share technique helps students develop confidence in their ability to express their mathematical thinking and share ideas with the class by first preparing and rehearsing in a lower-stakes environment.

Think-Pair-Rehearse-Share: a structure that gives students private think time and opportunities for them to both formulate their mathematical thinking and practice explaining that thinking in a small-group setting before sharing with the whole class

WHAT IS THINK-PAIR-REHEARSE-SHARE?

You may have heard of Think-Pair-Share (e.g., Kaddoura, 2013; Lyman, 1981) or even used the technique in your classroom. How is Think-Pair-Rehearse-Share different? In many ways, the two techniques are similar. Both give students time to think about a challenging math question or problem on their own before talking in pairs and then finally sharing their mathematical reasoning with the whole group. Think-Pair-Rehearse-Share is different because the Rehearse step of the technique gives students a dedicated opportunity to formulate their mathematical thinking and practice presenting their ideas with a partner, building confidence before sharing in a larger group setting.

THINK ABOUT IT

Have you used Think-Pair-Share or a similar technique as part of your literacy instruction? What might be different about using Think-Pair-Rehearse-Share in math lessons?

WHY MIGHT YOU USE THINK-PAIR-REHEARSE-SHARE?

For many students, sharing ideas in front of a large group can be intimidating. This is especially true for emergent multilingual learners. You know how important it is for students to feel safe and comfortable taking risks in your classroom, and creating this kind of discourse community isn't always easy. Think-Pair-Rehearse-Share is a technique that can be used any time you believe students would benefit from individual think time and collaboration with peers. The opportunity to think on their own, discuss their thinking with a partner, and then rehearse what they plan to say can help students feel safe expressing their ideas as part of a discourse community. In this way, using the Think-Pair-Rehearse-Share technique can support students in developing a sense of identity and authority as mathematical thinkers with ideas worth sharing.

Purposes of Think-Pair-Rehearse-Share

- Provide individual thinking time for students
- Create a safe environment for all students to share
- Allow for practice before presenting to a larger audience
- Enhance participation in the discourse community

GETTING STARTED WITH THINK-PAIR-REHEARSE-SHARE

To implement the Think-Pair-Rehearse-Share technique, use the following steps:

1. Introduce the task and make it clear to students what they should be thinking about. Make sure students are ready to engage with the mathematical work of the task.
2. Provide independent think time for students to consider their own ideas before discussing them with a partner. It may be helpful to have students record their thoughts using words, drawings, or equations (e.g., on paper or white boards).

3. Before students talk in pairs, give clear instructions for what they should be discussing and how to collaborate. For example, are they talking about possible strategies for solving the problem? Answers to the problem? What should they do after each partner has had a turn? Make sure to set the expectation that both students will have a turn to talk and listen.

4. Circulate and listen to the students' conversations. Take note of their mathematical ideas and explanations so you can purposefully select and sequence a few pairs to share their thinking with the whole class.

5. Give students time to rehearse their mathematical explanations with their partner before presenting them to the whole class. This step is especially important for emergent multilingual learners and other emergent math communicators who will benefit from extra practice to develop confidence in sharing their presentations.

6. Invite student pairs to share their mathematical ideas with the whole class during the Discuss phase of the lesson. Depending on your purpose, you may have all pairs share, or you may intentionally select and sequence a few pairs to share.

SUPPORTS THAT HELP WITH THINK-PAIR-REHEARSE-SHARE

Think-Pair-Rehearse-Share is a fairly straightforward technique to implement; however, your students will still need supports and scaffolds to learn how to productively engage in the process. Here are some ideas you can try.

Make instructions visible. Display instructions for the task in a place where students can refer to them during each step of the technique. Make the instructions for each step clear so students know what to do.

Wait to assign partners. Students often need support in understanding the expectations for the Think part of the technique so they use the time productively. It's common for students to want to jump right into talking with their partners without taking time to think quietly on their own. If you find that this is challenging for your students, wait to tell them who their partners will be or even that you plan to have them work in pairs until after they've had time to think individually.

Signal transitions. Use a signal or timer to clearly indicate the transitions between each part of the Think-Pair-Rehearse-Share technique. Set a specific amount of time for each part to keep the process moving and to ensure that students are working productively through each step.

Model expectations. As with Think time, make sure students understand norms for turn taking and the expectations for the steps of Pair (e.g., that each partner should have a turn to share) and Rehearse (e.g., that both partners should practice how they will present). You may want to model what it looks and sounds like to talk about mathematical ideas with a partner, including how to be an active listener and what to listen for, so students know what kind of discourse you expect.

Use sentence starters. Providing sentence starters can be especially helpful for formulating ideas during the Rehearse step.

SIGNS OF SUCCESS

- Students think quietly and write or draw their ideas during independent think time.

- Students discuss their mathematical thinking, explanations, and solution strategies in pairs, spending roughly equal time talking and listening.

- Students rehearse and are prepared to share ideas confidently during the whole-group discussion.

CAUTION SIGNALS

- Students are off-task or talk to their peers during independent think time. (Model and reinforce expectations, such as writing or drawing to record their thinking.)

- Students in pairs spend unequal time talking and listening. (Emphasize norms for turn-taking, and provide supports for all students to participate.)

IMPROVING AND ADAPTING THINK-PAIR-REHEARSE-SHARE

The following ideas will support you in going deeper with and extending this technique.

Share in groups of four. So far, we have focused on how to use Think-Pair-Rehearse-Share during the Explore phase to help students be ready for the Discuss phase, but moving into a whole-class discussion does not always need to be the case. After students finish rehearsing their ideas in pairs, combine each pair of students with another pair for the Share step. In this adaptation, students share their thinking in a group of four rather than with the whole class, and these groups can become the students' small groups for further work in the Explore phase.

Ask Probing and Pressing Math Questions. You can also combine Think-Pair-Rehearse-Share with the Probing and Pressing Math Questions technique (Chapter 15). To do this, listen to students' conversations as they talk in pairs and think about the kinds of questions you might want to ask during the Discuss phase. Then let specific students know what questions you plan to ask them about their work or their thinking. Students can practice their responses to these questions as they rehearse with a partner in preparation for the whole-group discussion.

EXAMINE PRACTICE

This vignette is a continuation of Ms. Ladeaux's lesson presented in Chapter 6, and for this reason, some elements of her planning are repeated. As you read the vignette below, ask yourself: How did Ms. Ladeaux address student mistakes when using the Think-Pair-Rehearse-Share technique?

Think-Pair-Rehearse-Share in Ms. Ladeaux's Kindergarten Classroom

Planning the Lesson

After 13 years teaching first grade, I am in my first year teaching Kindergarten. My story shares my experience launching a lesson on addition and subtraction within 10 using Story Problem Retelling. My class had been exploring the idea that adding or subtracting the number 1 gives the next, or the prior, number on the counting sequence. We also worked with adding or subtracting 2. So in this lesson I wanted to build on that learning as we worked with bigger numbers within 10. My math goal was for students to realize there are many strategies they can use to solve addition or subtraction problems within 10.

My discourse goals related to the listening and explaining dimensions of the Matrix. I wanted my students to be active listeners whether I was talking, their partner was talking, or someone was sharing with the whole class. I also wanted students to explain their mathematical thinking throughout the lesson.

I selected two result-unknown story problems for this lesson: one that required students to add 3 + 7 and one that was 4 + 3.

> There were 3 bees buzzing in the hive.
>
> Then 7 more bees joined them.
>
> How many bees are in the hive now?

> There were 4 bugs sitting on a vine.
>
> Then 3 more bugs joined them.
>
> How many bugs are on the vine now?

(continued)

EXAMINE PRACTICE (continued)

I wanted the class to work on the problems one at a time, doing two rounds of Launch-Explore-Discuss in the lesson. I had planned that, if it went well, we would work on a change-unknown problem as a whole class at the end, during the Discuss phase, and use Story Problem Retelling together one more time. The problem structure was $3 + \underline{} = 7$. We would have just discussed a problem that was about $4 + 3 = 7$, so I thought it could go well.

I decided to use Think-Pair-Rehearse-Share for the Explore phase because I wanted students to discuss what they knew and what they needed to solve the problem. Then I wanted them to actually solve the problem and prepare to share their solution strategies. My goal for the Explore phase was to scaffold students' engagement with responsive discourse and let them practice for their presentation of ideas. The Share part of this technique was going to be part of my Discuss phase for this lesson.

Enacting the Lesson

During each round of the Explore phase, I had the pairs work together on their ideas, and I was pleased to see students deciding to use a variety of tools to solve the problems, such as white boards, unit cubes, counters, story mats, or number lines. "With your partner," I said, "you can get the materials you need and find a place you want to sit. Make sure you work as a pair to implement your ideas and get ready to present your solutions. Make sure to rehearse what you are going to say about what you did."

As I walked around the room, most pairs found the answer 10 for the first problem really quickly. I asked them to make sure they had labeled their solutions, double-checked their work, and were rehearsing to share how they solved it. For example, one pair produced a representation that had numbers separated by a line. When I asked them what they had done, they said, "We showed 3 and a break apart line and we had 7 more. That is 10." When I asked them to explain more, they suggested there were 3 bees and then 7 more bees came to make 10 bees total. I kept pressing, and they said they used 3 and 7 make 10. I liked that they were thinking of "make 10."

When we used Think-Pair-Rehearse-Share for the second problem, students had thought carefully about the problem and mapped their solution strategies. In their pairs, they solved the problem correctly with no trouble and relatively quickly. They also planned together for what they wanted to share and took the initiative to rehearse their presentations together. There were several representations for the problem this time, so there was enough richness in the students' work for a good discussion to happen. After this Explore phase, I knew students were ready for the Discuss phase.

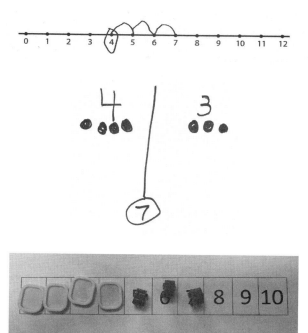

(continued)

EXAMINE PRACTICE (continued)

Reflecting on the Explore Phase

As I walked around during the Explore phase, I saw so many different ways the students were approaching the problems. And I really saw all of them participating. They made sense of the problems as they worked in pairs, which was my goal, and they were able to come up with solutions and prepare for a great discussion. I learned a lot about how they were constructing their mathematical arguments. One group used unit cubes to organize their 7 as a row of 5 and a row of 2, as if they had a 10-frame. When I asked them why, they said it was easier to see the number 7 that way. I thought that was pretty cool, and I asked them to rehearse this idea to share with the class.

One pair had made a mistake counting on from 4 but counting the 4 a second time, so they only reached 6. They fixed it during their rehearsal. This happens sometimes—while the students are rehearsing what they will share with the group, they self-correct. There are times that they don't, and that is okay with me. In these cases, I try to make sure that groups with mistakes are among the groups I call on to share their findings. Then I can see who agrees with them, questions them, or disagrees. I had this pair of students share their mistake and how they fixed it. This is where the discourse really takes off and students usually learn from their mistakes. That is why it's so important during the Explore phase for me to take a back seat. I usually walk around and ask questions, but I try not to disturb the flow of what the partners are doing. Building a safe community helps students be risk takers. Even when they make a mistake, they usually realize what they did incorrectly without freezing up, and then they can correct on the spot and still share out their findings. I think that is pretty cool.

Examining Ms. Ladeaux's Explore Phase

This example of a productive Explore phase shows students using several different representations to solve math problems after having individual think time and discussing their ideas with a partner during Think-Pair-

Rehearse-Share. Ms. Ladeaux uses the Explore phase to monitor students' reasoning and argumentations, and she selects pairs for sharing during the Discuss phase, while deciding how to address mistakes. She helps students prepare for the sharing by asking questions, which allows them to sharpen their presentations. Using Think-Pair-Rehearse-Share in the Explore phase, Ms. Ladeaux has the class ready for a productive Discuss phase, when they continue to participate in high-quality discourse and address mistakes the teacher identified during the Explore phase.

DISCUSS WITH COLLEAGUES

1   What aspects of implementing the Think-Pair-Rehearse-Share technique might be most challenging for you and your students?

2   What norms do you think are important to have in place in order for students to successfully engage in Think-Pair-Rehearse-Share?

3   What are some factors you might think about when deciding how to pair students together, such as students' varying mathematical and linguistic strengths?

CONNECT TO YOUR PRACTICE

Use the Think-Pair-Rehearse-Share technique in one of your math lessons. As you plan, think about specific ideas you would like to emerge in the whole-group discussion and how you might select and sequence the order in which pairs of students share those ideas. During the lesson, actively listen for those ideas and give students time to rehearse them before sharing.

NOTES

_____

_____

_____

_____

_____

_____

_____

_____

_____

_____

_____

_____

_____

_____

Math Four Square

Venn diagrams. Storyboards. Frayer model. Chances are you have heard of these graphic organizers and perhaps even used one of them in your teaching. They are often used across the content areas to help students organize their thinking, keep track of and even sequence multiple ideas, and highlight important comparisons or connections among ideas. In literacy, the Four Square (Brunn, 2002) supports students' abilities to process ideas in reading, illustrate related attributes of a context, and understand the relationships among literacy concepts by presenting the information spatially. Similarly, in our work, the Math Four Square technique helps students process and represent their mathematical thinking while connecting across different representations.

WHAT IS MATH FOUR SQUARE?

Math Four Square is a graphic organizer designed to promote students' use of multiple representations in problem solving and facilitate the exploration of mathematical relationships among ideas. As the name suggests, the Math Four Square is divided into four labeled quadrants (Figure 10-1). In the top left quadrant, students indicate what they are trying to figure out to solve the problem, that is, the question they are answering. The other three quadrants are assigned to different representations of students' mathematical thinking and solutions: pictures, numbers, and words. As students work on the problem, they create and use multiple representations to communicate their thinking and recognize connections among mathematical ideas.

Math Four Square: a graphic organizer that promotes students' use of multiple representations in problem solving and facilitates the exploration of mathematical relationships among ideas

Figure 10-1 ◆ Math Four Square

🐞 Question	Show with pictures 🐿
5 Show with numbers	Tell with words ✏️

WHY MIGHT YOU USE MATH FOUR SQUARE?

Working with and accommodating students with various communication preferences within one lesson can be hard because students have different strengths and needs. Tied to the explaining and modes of communication dimensions of the Math Discourse Matrix (Figure 1-2), Math Four Square allows the teacher to accommodate students' different preferences while also exposing them to several alternative representations of mathematical ideas. Asking students to complete all the squares or their favorite squares gives the teacher a glimpse into their mathematical thinking.

THINK ABOUT IT

How can Math Four Square be used to informally assess students' work and mathematical understanding?

Let's take a look at a third-grade task and how a teacher might use Math Four Square to help students examine relationships among mathematical representations.

Mr. Franklin's class is planting trees in the school yard. They bought 30 trees. They want them in rows with the same number of trees in each row. There needs to be between 2 and 10 trees in each row. How can the 30 trees be organized?

Third-grade students may use various solutions and representations when solving this problem. In this class, the teacher asked each student to complete all squares before discussing their solution with a peer and deciding which squares to share with the class. Figure 10-2 shows one student's completed Math Four Square.

Figure 10-2 • Math Four Square Example

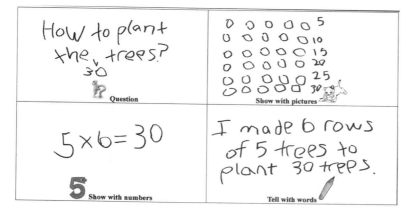

Asking this student to show where the rows of trees are in the picture would be a good question to connect the picture to the words. This student can also compare work with another student who is thinking 3 rows of 10 trees to discuss the mathematical similarities and differences highlighted in each of their representations. More broadly, the teacher may ask student pairs to discuss how the numbers they used are displayed in their pictures (e.g., Where do you see the 5 and 6 in the picture? What do they represent?). Doing so pushes students to look for important mathematical relationships that then further their conceptual understanding of ideas.

Purposes of Math Four Square

- Accommodate students' communication preferences
- Bring forth different representations for discussion
- Foster mathematical connections among representations

GETTING STARTED WITH MATH FOUR SQUARE

The representations or strategies you expect your students to use while completing a Math Four Square should be ones that can be communicated visually with pictures, symbols, and words. Before implementing the Math Four Square technique, it is important to anticipate possible student representations and the mathematical connections among them. This will help you prepare guiding questions that facilitate student understanding of those connections and highlight them during the whole-group discussion.

To implement the Math Four Square technique, use the following steps:

1. Distribute enough materials for students to think through, solve, and represent their thinking. Generally, it would be useful for students to have the following:
    *   a paper or poster paper with a printed or drawn Math Four Square organizer
    *   markers or colored pencils, in several colors, for preparing the representations
    *   manipulative materials to use when working out the problem (Be careful to choose manipulatives that students can later represent with ease in their Math Four Square organizer.)
2. Have students talk in groups to first discuss the problem and make sense of the question they need to answer. Then indicate to students it is good to brainstorm ideas before filling in the Math Four Square. Their math discourse should be about unpacking the task, what they are being asked, and how they might solve the problem and represent their thinking.
3. Instruct students to begin filling in the Math Four Square individually, in pairs, or in groups. They should start at the top left quadrant to ensure they understand the math question posed. From there, students can work with the remaining quadrants in any order.
4. Monitor students' progress as they work. You may use this time to make note of ideas you would like to address in the Discuss phase. For example, you might document interesting student ideas or representations to share, in particular those that lend themselves to highlighting important mathematical relationships.

5. Check in with students and ask guiding questions about how they are thinking about the problem, using Math Four Square to communicate their ideas, and solving the problem. For example:

- *How did you get started on this problem?*
- *What do these numbers mean in your representation?*
- *Is there another way you can show that?*
- *What mathematical relationships do you see between your picture and the equation?*

SUPPORTS THAT HELP WITH MATH FOUR SQUARE

The following ideas can help support students' success with the Math Four Square technique:

Demonstrate expectations. To begin, it is important that students understand your expectations for what type of information goes in each quadrant and how that information can be used to explore and share ideas. You can incorporate one quadrant at a time into your instruction until you are able to model how to fill in the entire Math Four Square. Then you can model how to share the mathematical thinking that is represented in the different squares as well as the relationships among different representations. For example, using the work shown in Figure 10-2, you could discuss how the equation $5 \times 6 = 30$ is represented in the picture the student drew and how it connects or relates to a student who used the equation $3 \times 10 = 30$ or $2 \times 15 = 30$.

Use with Task Think-Aloud. If students are struggling to make sense of the task and determine what they are trying to solve for, you may consider pairing Math Four Square with the Task Think-Aloud technique (Chapter 7) to model how you are thinking about the information in the problem. For example, you could talk about how the quadrants in the organizer helped you think through and reason about the problem.

Additional supports include providing a math word bank of relevant vocabulary, sentence starters, or possible solution strategies for student reference. For example, if using the earlier tree planting problem, you might offer words such as *arrays, rows, columns, multiplication,* or *skip counting.* You could also provide sentence starters such as "I planted … rows of … trees …" or "When I compare my picture and my numbers …."

> **THINK ABOUT IT**
>
> How might you adapt Math Four Square for students who cannot yet write?

SIGNS OF SUCCESS

- Students demonstrate their mathematical thinking in different ways.

- Students describe mathematical relationships among different representations.

- Students use relevant vocabulary when describing their work.

CAUTION SIGNALS

- Students are not attending to the question they need to answer. (Remind them to always start the Math Four Square in the top left quadrant.)

- Students struggle to move beyond the representation that they feel most comfortable with. (Try using the Task Think-Aloud technique to model different ways to represent the problem.)

- Students are not able to make connections among their different representations. (Consider using sentence starters to focus students' thinking on the underlying mathematical ideas.)

IMPROVING AND ADAPTING MATH FOUR SQUARE

Once Math Four Square becomes routine in your classroom, you can modify your expectations for each quadrant based on your purposes for the activity. Here are a few examples of how the quadrants can be modified.

Words quadrant. The words quadrant can serve many purposes based on the lesson goals. Students can write their final answer in words, use words to describe how they solved the problem, or identify the important academic vocabulary in the problem. In addition, your expectations for how students fill in this quadrant can vary based on the language and writing skills of individual students. Students can record a few words, use invented spellings, or replace some words with pictures as they are developing their language and writing skills. Allowing emergent multilingual learners to write in any language they know can also support the expression of their mathematical knowledge.

Pictures quadrant. The expectations for the pictures quadrant also can vary based on your lesson goals and the task that is being explored. For instance, the third-grade task shared earlier about Mr. Franklin planting trees instructed students to plant the trees in equal rows—this can make the picture easier. Students can explore with manipulatives and then draw their final representation in the pictures quadrant. You can also include a printed template for the type of visual you would like them to use, like a number line or a ten-frame, so they do not have to redraw their representations.

Numbers quadrant. The numbers quadrant gives students the opportunity to extract their numerical understandings from the context of the problem. Students can represent the problem using an equation (as shown in Figure 10-2), a table, operations or algorithms, or showing their counting numbers. You may also decide to change the use of the quadrants in a more targeted way. For example, you can have students represent the solution to the problem as a table in quadrant 2, a graph in quadrant 3, and an equation in quadrant 4.

Sharing ideas. Students should have a clear understanding of how they will share their work during the Discuss phase. Offering time for students to rehearse their presentations is helpful. You can ask groups to share just one or two quadrants and carefully sequence the presentations to promote comparisons of similarities and differences in representations and approaches.

EXAMINE PRACTICE

When reading the vignette below, consider what Ms. Sonder did while students were working on their Math Four Square to ensure they understood the different ways they could solve addition problems with three addends. How did she scaffold student work during the Explore phase?

(continued)

EXAMINE PRACTICE (continued)

Math Four Square in Ms. Sonder's First-Grade Classroom

Planning the Lesson

I have been teaching for 20 years, and this is my eighth year teaching first grade. For this lesson, I wanted my first graders to solve an addition story problem with three addends. This is the problem we worked on:

> Ben was cleaning up the room.
>
> He found 6 yellow pencils, 4 blue pencils, and 7 red pencils on the floor.
>
> How many pencils did Ben find?

I wanted my students to realize they can solve this problem in different ways. I also wanted them to focus on their explanations and use various representations and modes of communication—these were my discourse goals from the Matrix. I planned to use Math Four Square during the Explore phase because I thought this technique would highlight the different ways in which students represent both the problem and their mathematical thinking. Math Four Square promotes mathematical connections and the use of representations, which was my goal.

I planned to read the problem during the Launch and go over Math Four Square with students to remind them of how to work on it. I decided I would have students work with a partner and ask each student to complete two of the four squares to make sure both partners were able to share their own mathematical thinking and to analyze the mathematical thinking of another student. Finally, I wanted to conclude using the Math Learning Summary (Chapter 16) in the Discuss phase.

Enacting the Lesson

Twenty students were gathered on the carpet as I launched the lesson. They started working on Math Four Square with their partners during the Explore phase. When I was walking around, I saw that most pairs had written the question: "How many pencils did Ben find?" That was good. Many groups used different colored circles to represent the pencils, and one group drew actual pencils for the pictures. It was interesting to see that some pairs labeled the groups, like 6, 4, 7, and others labeled each pencil, from 1 to 17, as a way to count all. The Show With Numbers square was the most interesting to me as I was monitoring. A couple of pairs used number lines. Some students showed how they were counting on, which is something we have been practicing, and they wrote 7 and then up to 17. I had a couple of pairs write the equation 6 + 4 + 7 = 17, which was great and I decided I was definitely selecting that one for presentation during the Discuss phase.

One of my groups had the answer 16, and I asked them to tell me more about their strategy. They couldn't quite explain it to me, so I asked them to talk further about the problem and what they were trying to do. Later I saw they had changed their answer to 17 and I asked them to tell me more about their strategy. This time, they could actually tell me what they had done: "We started with 6 and counted on, then put 4, then put 7 and drawed them and got 17." Most groups wrote statements like this for the Tell With Words square.

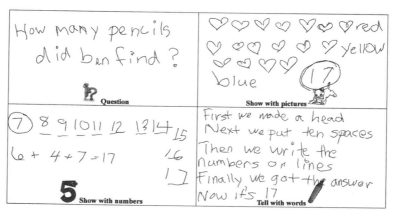

(continued)

EXAMINE PRACTICE (continued)

There was one pair of emergent multilingual learners working together. When I got to them, they had not yet written their statement on the Tell With Words square. I asked them what they had done, and we worked together to use their words to create a sentence to write. I then asked them to practice saying that sentence to each other so that they could share during the discussion. I let them know I was going to ask them to share, which is something I like to do to ensure all my students are prepared for the discussion.

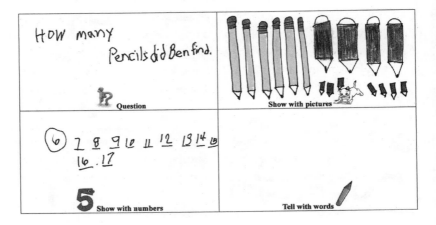

Reflecting on the Explore Phase

Overall, I think the students were successful with the discourse goal because of how they were engaged and participating. Most of them could solve the addition problems with three addends with no real difficulty. I consider my Explore phase highly successful because that is when most of the responsive discourse occurred. All but one set of partners were able to use multiple modes of communication and completed the task of solving, representing, and writing about the story problem. The students who had a harder time were deeply involved in the Show With Pictures square, and they were neatly drawing pencils and coloring them with great detail, so they did not complete all the work. This tells me they still need to represent every unit, which is something for us to work on. I was concerned they would lose focus on the task, so I reread the story problem to refocus their attention. In a follow-up lesson, I will consider assigning partners instead of letting students choose. This would be one good way to support students in making progress, and it can also help my emergent math communicators.

My students enjoyed using Math Four Square, and it gave me a great way to see how they were making sense of and representing the story problem. I also liked that I could help students who were having a harder time writing what to say with words, allowing them to prepare a sentence to share. Although they did not write it down independently, they were able to tell what they did with words.

Examining Ms. Sonder's Explore Phase

With Math Four Square, Ms. Sonder can see students' work during the Explore phase and help them build their mathematical argumentation. Students model their thinking through multiple modes of communication, allowing the teacher to examine their ideas and ways of representing them during the Explore phase. This vignette shows the power of this technique to highlight student thinking and where individuals might need further support. Ms. Sonder purposefully addresses the pros and cons of this Explore phase in the reflection, preparing for further work that will allow all students to engage with the math of the lesson and with high-quality discourse.

DISCUSS WITH COLLEAGUES

1   How can a completed Math Four Square be used to help students discuss the mathematical connections among their different representations?

2   Choose a math problem from your instructional materials that could be solved using Math Four Square. Together fill out a few Math Four Square charts with different ways students may represent the math in the task. Discuss the mathematical relationships among those representations.

CONNECT TO YOUR PRACTICE

Plan a two-day lesson where students complete Math Four Square on the first day and engage in the mathematical discussion on the second day. Collect the Math Four Square sheets, analyze them, and select and sequence two or three to use during the discussion.

☐   Which Math Four Squares did you select? What important mathematical ideas (related to the lesson goals) do they convey?

☐   What questions will you ask students in order to elicit connections among the mathematical representations shared?

☐   How will you sequence the discussion to help students make those connections and develop understanding of the important mathematical ideas?

NOTES

_____

_____

_____

Talk Triangle

Have you ever noticed that the students in your small groups aren't actually speaking or listening to one another during their group work time? Oftentimes, it's not that students *don't want* to talk, but that they aren't sure *how* to talk and listen in small groups. This dilemma is not unique to discussions in math; students are just as likely to need help knowing how to talk in reading and other subjects. The Talk Triangle (Luxford & Smart, 2009) provides students with scaffolding and roles for small-group discussions to help the conversation start flowing productively.

WHAT IS TALK TRIANGLE?

The Talk Triangle technique is designed to give each student a specific role in small-group discourse in order to make group work time productive and meaningful. It helps students talk to their peers about their mathematical thinking and reasoning while also supporting them in listening carefully to one another. As you might guess, the Talk Triangle is made up of three students taking on the roles of Talker, Listener, and Questioner. These roles go deeper than some of the oft-used group roles such as timekeeper or materials manager because they are meant to support students' argumentation in math. The initial roles help students learn how to contribute meaningfully to small-group mathematical discussions, with the intention that, over time, the assignment of roles becomes less necessary and students become confident and adept at talking together about math problems.

Talk Triangle: a structure that gives each member a specific discourse role in order to make small-group discussions productive and meaningful

The Talk Triangle roles are defined as follows:

- The **Talker** is essentially the problem doer. They read the problem aloud and share, both in words and in other modes (e.g., drawing, writing, gesturing), how they are approaching the problem. The Talker should expect to respond to questions from the Questioner and receive help in doing so from the Listener.

- The **Listener** pays careful attention to what the Talker is doing and saying. They should be prepared to restate anything the Talker has said. The Listener also responds to questions from the Questioner.

  - The **Questioner** is responsible for asking relevant math questions of both the Talker and the Listener. The Questioner may ask questions when the Talker is stuck or pauses, or may ask questions for clarification or justification.

THINK ABOUT IT

Do you ever assign roles to students working in small groups? If so, what kinds of roles are they? How do they compare with the Talk Triangle roles?

WHY MIGHT YOU USE TALK TRIANGLE?

Picture this: A third-grade teacher provides her students with an engaging math task with multiple entry points and solution strategies. The teacher purposefully groups the students based on how they solved other problems in the past in an attempt to generate multiple strategies for discussion in each group. Before they start working, the teacher tells them that during their group work time they should talk to one another, decide together how to solve, and then create a group product with their solution. While circulating, the teacher notices that in most groups the students are solving the problem individually, and then each student takes a turn sharing their work with the group. The students' discussions are purely procedural and they do not respond to one another, comment on each other's strategies, or ask each other questions. In a few groups, the students have different answers but do not seem to notice or acknowledge it. The teacher is disappointed by what is taking place in the groups; despite specifically encouraging students to talk to each other and use one another's ideas, that did not occur. Even with best intentions, without clear expectations and purposeful organization to promote discourse, group work may result in students only sharing procedures without explanation or justification, or not interacting much at all.

Purposes of Talk Triangle

- Provide structure for students to share their thinking and reasoning about a problem
- Help peers consider each other's mathematical ideas
- Organize students to listen to, explore, and explain others' mathematical ideas
- Foster relevant questions that clarify or expand others' mathematical ideas

Using the Talk Triangle technique during the Explore phase will help students learn how to talk, question, and listen to each other in ways that support high-quality discourse and deepen understanding.

GETTING STARTED WITH TALK TRIANGLE

Students should be familiar with each of the roles prior to working in a Talk Triangle. In addition to describing the roles to students, it can be helpful to demonstrate and practice the roles before using them. Consider engaging students with a single role one day and then focusing on another role the next. This process allows students to understand each role before having small groups take on the three roles at once. It may also be helpful to provide role cards with expectations and sentence or question starters, especially as students are first becoming comfortable with the roles.

Once students are prepared to participate in Talk Triangles on their own, there are four main steps to implementing the technique in your classroom:

1. Assign students to groups of three. You may consider creating groups initially so that each one has a student who is confident with each role.
2. Assign the three roles. Roles can be assigned ahead of time, or students can select for themselves. Make sure all students, including emergent multilinguals and emergent math communicators, have a chance over time

to participate in all three roles. The roles are a chance to build on each student's strengths and help them develop in other areas. If working on more than one task during a class period, you may choose to have students rotate through the roles.

3. Set expectations. Assign students a task to work on with their Talk Triangles, and inform students of the expectations for their work time. For example, is the Talk Triangle time meant only for discussing thinking, or will it lead to creating a product together?

4. Monitor group discourse. As you circulate, recognize and emphasize the contributions of each role in productive math conversations.

A sample fifth-grade story problem and the resulting Talk Triangle dialogue follow:

SCENARIO 11-1

There are 30 students in Mr. Zhou's class: $\frac{3}{5}$ are wearing shorts, $\frac{1}{3}$ are wearing pants, and the rest are wearing skirts. What fraction represents the number of students wearing skirts?

Talker: Okay, so we know that there are 30 kids in the class. So first I think I should figure out how many is $\frac{3}{5}$. Well, what would $\frac{1}{5}$ be? Hmmm . . . 30 divided by 5 is 6. So $\frac{1}{5}$ is 6.

Questioner: How does knowing $\frac{1}{5}$ help you?

Talker: If we know $\frac{1}{5}$ we can find $\frac{3}{5}$. We know that $\frac{1}{5}$ of 30 is 6, but we want $\frac{3}{5}$. So if $\frac{1}{5}$ is 6, then $\frac{2}{5}$ is 2 × 6, and then $\frac{3}{5}$ is 3 × 6. And that is 18.

Listener: Okay, so 18 kids are wearing shorts. Let's write that down so we don't forget.

Talker: $\frac{1}{3}$ are wearing pants. That's easy. $\frac{1}{3}$ of 30 is 10, because 10 + 10 + 10 is 30.

Listener: Okay, let me see if I understood what you said. 18 students,

which is the same as $\frac{3}{5}$, are wearing shorts. And 10 is $\frac{1}{3}$ of 30, so 10 students are wearing pants.

Talker: Yeah, so 2 students are wearing skirts.

Questioner: How do you know 2 are wearing skirts?

Talker: Well, because 18 are wearing shorts, plus 10 are wearing pants. That's 28, right? And there are 30 kids total in the class. So 30 minus 28 is 2, which is the number of students wearing skirts. But we aren't done yet until we find the fraction.

Questioner: What do you mean, find the fraction?

Talker: Well, the question doesn't ask how many students are wearing skirts. It asks the fraction of students wearing skirts. There were 2 out of 30 wearing skirts, so the fraction is $\frac{2}{30}$, or $\frac{1}{15}$.

Questioner: Can you say more about that?

Talker: Sure. I see that the numerator is 2 and the denominator is an even number. So I can divide both by 2. That gives me $\frac{1}{15}$ of the class is wearing skirts.

Listener: So we found out there are 18 kids wearing shorts, 10 wearing pants, and 2 wearing skirts. If we want the fractions of students wearing skirts, that is $\frac{2}{30}$, which is $\frac{1}{15}$ if we simplify it.

In the sample dialogue, you'll notice that all three students were meaningfully involved in the discussion. All three students played a role in thinking about the problem and forming an explanation of the solution. The Talk Triangle may not lead to groups having discussions like this right away, but with practice and support, students will learn to use talking, listening, and questioning productively in their conversations.

SUPPORTS THAT HELP WITH TALK TRIANGLE

Students will benefit from learning about the Talk Triangle roles and the structure of a Talk Triangle conversation. In addition to preparing students to play each of the roles, the following ideas can help support students' success with the Talk Triangle technique:

Sentence starters. It can be helpful to have some "stock" language that students can use to get the conversation going. Starters such as "The problem is asking us to . . ." and "The first way I want to try to solve this problem is . . ." can help the Talker explain their thinking in real time. The Listener might be helped with sentence starters such as "What I heard you say is . . ." or "You know that . . . because . . . ." You'll find that most sentence starters can be applied to many different tasks, but you may want to add task-specific ones as well.

Question starters. Similarly, offer the Questioner starters such as "How did you figure out . . ." and "What did you mean when you said . . . ." Questions to ask the Listener might be "Can you explain . . . in another way?" and "What important ideas did you hear?" Similar to sentence starters, there are general question starters for many tasks, and you may want to include some task-specific ones to emphasize key mathematical ideas. Your question starters might suggest what sentence starters would help the Talker and Listener respond to the Questioner.

Modeling. Demonstrating each role reinforces expectations and helps students see the roles in action. For example, you may model how to use the question and sentence starters to start the conversation and keep it moving productively. You could also use a script of a sample Talk Triangle and have students act it out for the rest of the class.

SIGNS OF SUCCESS

- Emergent multilingual learners and emergent math communicators contribute meaningfully to the Talk Triangle.

- Students ask questions of each other with purpose, rather than just reading them from a list.

- Students listen carefully to one another and respond to what is being said.

CAUTION SIGNALS

- The most outgoing students are Talkers in every lesson, while typically reserved students are always Listeners. (Assign Talk Triangle roles ahead of time.)

- Students tend to work individually and then have superficial discussions at the end of group work. (Consider having checkpoints throughout the Talk Triangle to help keep students on task.)

IMPROVING AND ADAPTING TALK TRIANGLE

Once you are comfortable with the basic steps of the Talk Triangle, there are a few recommendations for how to better prepare for and use this technique with students, including ideas for adaptation.

Monitor. Even with experience and supports, you should monitor students in Talk Triangles to ensure that they are successful with each role and in their discourse overall. You might use a monitoring sheet as you circulate to note each student's involvement in discussions and how effectively they use each of the roles. Point out when students are engaged in their roles productively to set the norms for the discourse you value.

Ensure students try all roles. It may be tempting to let your most eager students choose the Talker role and less forthcoming students play the Listener role. Over time, it is important that *all* students experience *all* roles. Encourage students to use their assets in each role. The Talker role is ideal for students to try out academic language. Listeners have opportunities to focus on a peer's thinking. Questioners get a chance to ask their peers for explanations and justifications about the mathematical arguments they construct.

Use Talk Squares. Depending on the number of students in your class, you may find an occasion to use Talk Squares, in which you create an additional role or you can have two students share one of the roles. Talk Squares are useful when a student needs support with one of the roles. A particularly challenging or complex problem may also be a time to consider using two Talkers.

Talk without a Talk Triangle. Finally, it is important to remember that the Talk Triangle is a formal structure to help students learn how to engage in responsive discourse. After students are comfortable with the role expectations, you should encourage these parts of productive discourse—explaining, listening, and questioning—whether or not you are using the Talk Triangle formally. Doing so, you begin to establish important socio-mathematical norms in your classroom.

EXAMINE PRACTICE

In the vignette that follows, Ms. Szabo uses scaffolds before students implement Talk Triangles in their small groups. Although many of Ms. Szabo's students engage in productive conversations during the Explore phase, there are still a few students who struggle. What more could Ms. Szabo do to set all students up for success?

Talk Triangle in Practice in Ms. Szabo's Third-Grade Classroom

Planning the Lesson

I am a third-grade teacher, and although I have been teaching early elementary grades for 15 years, this is only my second year teaching third grade. My story is about a lesson in which I wanted students to apply their understanding of the operations to solve two-step story problems. We had worked on many one-step problems, and I wanted my students to realize that they can set up a two-step problem as one problem only, or they can solve it one step at a time. So I used a worksheet of two-step problems that our district provided for teachers.

Only last year I started having discourse goals for my lessons. For this lesson, I wanted to help students improve their listening because that is a skill that they have struggled with this year. This is perhaps the hardest of the dimensions in the Matrix for my students. I planned to launch the lesson using Math Bet Lines. Then I wanted my students to use the Talk Triangle as they completed the worksheet during the Explore phase. I thought the Talk Triangle would be perfect for supporting listening because it provides a structure for students to explain their thinking, listen to their peers, and ask each other questions. I wanted the students to rotate roles in the Talk Triangle as they worked through the problems. I created question starters for the Questioner to use specifically with the Talker or with the Listener to scaffold the conversation.

Talker
How would you prove that?

What made you decide you needed to use _____?

Why did you choose that problem solving method?

Can you create a picture or model to show that?

_____

Listener
Can you solve the problem using a different strategy?

Can you explain what _____ has done so far? Is there anything else they need to do?

Can you repeat what _____ just said in your own words?

Do you agree or disagree with _____ and why?

Enacting the Lesson

My 21 students were sitting at their desks, arranged in a U shape, when we launched the work of the lesson. We then reviewed the roles for the Talk Triangle, and I handed out the task sheet and the question starters for the Questioners. I pre-assigned groups of three students with different assets and needs and allowed the groups to move into any space in the room, taking a white board and dry-erase markers. This is the first problem they worked on:

> Katie and Valerie are giving one apple to each person in their class. Katie has three bags of apples with 4 apples in each bag, and Valerie has two bags of apples with 7 apples in each bag. How many apples do they have?

As I was walking around, I could hear a lot of conversations in the groups. I heard one Listener tell their group, "I liked how you did the problem with equal groups because it can be confusing. I would be confused on this problem, and listening to your way helped." I tried to encourage Questioners and Listeners to be involved with the Talker and ask questions.

(continued)

EXAMINE PRACTICE (continued)

I modeled some questions for them, like "How do you think you are going to find out the answer to this problem?" and "Can you tell me how you got that?" I also helped some of the groups that were stuck; for example, one of the groups was adding numbers that needed to be multiplied, so I tried to work with the Questioner to make them think about the problem further. With some groups, I was trying to get them to use equations to represent what they were doing. Like a group that was adding 4 three times, I tried to get them to write a multiplication equation for that. There were lots of useful representations emerging from the small groups, which made me think that we would have productive discussions.

$$3 \times 4 = 12$$
$$7 \times 2 = 14$$

$$\begin{array}{r} 14 \\ +12 \\ \hline 26 \end{array}$$

$$10 + 10 = 20$$
$$4 + 2 = 6$$
$$20 + 6 = \boxed{26}$$

$$4 \times 3 + 7 \times 2 = 26$$

O O O O O   O O
O O   O
             O
             O
             O
             O
             O

Reflecting on the Explore Phase

While I was circulating, I could see that some of my groups definitely needed more support than others, so I tried to ask probing questions where I thought they were needed. I also noticed that the Questioners definitely needed the question starters I had provided. In many groups I supported the Questioners as I was walking around. Still, for the most part, I felt that the quality of the conversations among the students was strong. And I also saw evidence of students listening during the Explore phase and actually throughout the lesson, which was part of my discourse goal. I was pleased with that. In the end, students were unable to finish all the problems on the worksheet. Maybe I had too many. But I thought that was okay because I always think that quality supersedes quantity, and we had some very good mathematical discussions in this lesson about how to set up and solve two-step story problems.

Examining Ms. Szabo's Explore Phase

Students listening to each other is always an important discourse goal featuring a key dimension of the Math Discourse Matrix. Ms. Szabo uses the Talk Triangle to support students as they work in small groups and practice listening to each other. There is a particular focus on the Questioners, providing students in this role with question starters. The teacher monitors carefully to scaffold the use of probing questions that allow for the examination of abstract and quantitative reasoning. Pushing for high-quality discourse in small groups, Ms. Szabo sets the stage for productive discussions, which creates confidence that the math and discourse goals will be met as the lesson comes to a close in the Discuss phase.

DISCUSS WITH COLLEAGUES

1   What do small-group discussions typically look like in your classroom? Do all students in each group have a part to play? Do some students tend to "take a back seat"? What do you do to encourage participation from all students?

2   After you have tried the Talk Triangle, reflect on how the technique helps with establishing socio-mathematical norms in your classroom.

CONNECT TO PRACTICE

Use the Talk Triangle in one of your math lessons. Prior to the lesson, consider what aspects of each Talk Triangle role will be most challenging for your students. Plan supports or scaffolds you can use to help them be successful in their roles.

NOTES

_____

_____

_____

_____

_____

_____

_____

Solution Draft and Final Copy

When working on a writing assignment, students are encouraged to use the writing process to edit and revise their work. They begin by writing a draft, and then modify its organization and wording, and correct errors, to improve it based on feedback from the teacher or their peers, creating a final copy (e.g., Soto-Hinman & Hetzel, 2009; Tompkins, Campbell, Green, & Smith, 2014). In math, it's less common for students to approach their work in this way. The Solution Draft and Final Copy technique provides an opportunity for students to clarify, strengthen, and correct their mathematical thinking through discussions with peers and to create a final representation of their solution strategies for sharing with the class.

WHAT IS SOLUTION DRAFT AND FINAL COPY?

In Solution Draft and Final Copy, students jot down their initial mathematical ideas, revise those ideas as they work on the problem, and create more complete and organized versions of their mathematical thinking. Typically, pairs or small groups of students engage in Solution Draft and Final Copy during the Explore phase, collaborating on solving a math task in preparation for sharing their solution in the Discuss phase. The draft serves as a record of students' mathematical thinking while working on a math task. It includes brainstorming as well as several attempts, potentially successful and unsuccessful, to solve a math task. Based on the draft, students create the final copy, which is a clear and organized record of how they represented and solved the task. The final copy should be a product that stands alone, making students' mathematical thinking explicit, with little need for additional explanation.

Solution Draft and Final Copy: a process in which students record their initial mathematical ideas; strengthen, clarify, and correct their thinking; and create a more complete and organized representation of that thinking for sharing

WHY MIGHT YOU USE SOLUTION DRAFT AND FINAL COPY?

You may have students who think that solutions to math tasks are either "right" or "wrong," or who think that being skilled in math means that they will arrive at the correct answer on the first try. But when students work on challenging math tasks, they often need to rethink their work or try multiple approaches before determining a solution strategy that is viable and makes sense. The draft portion of Solution Draft and Final Copy supports students through this process, providing a structure where it is okay to try different approaches that may or may not be successful.

Even when students have successfully solved a math task, they may struggle to explain or represent their work. The final copy helps students carefully consider how to organize and display their mathematical reasoning and argument so that others can understand their approach. The final copy also helps you identify students' approaches so you can purposefully select and sequence whose work to highlight in the Discuss phase.

Purposes of Solution Draft and Final Copy

- Normalize aspects of productive struggle such as mistakes, dead ends, and false starts as part of the process of solving math problems
- Provide an opportunity for students to model with math and construct viable arguments
- Encourage work with peers to resolve discrepancies, make connections among approaches or representations, and come to a consensus about a solution to the task
- Help students clearly represent and articulate their mathematical reasoning

Accomplishing these purposes during the Explore phase prepares the class for the Discuss phase. Students will have a product that clearly displays their work that they can explain to the class, and you will have been able to select and sequence student presenters whose work highlights the central mathematical ideas of the lesson.

GETTING STARTED WITH SOLUTION DRAFT AND FINAL COPY

To implement the Solution Draft and Final Copy technique, use the following steps:

1. Communicate your expectations for both the draft and final copy. Depending on your students' needs, these expectations will vary.

2. Distribute Solution Draft and Final Copy materials to pairs or groups of students. Choose materials for the final copy based on how you plan to have students share work (e.g., projecting, posting on the wall). Solution Draft and Final Copy materials typically include the following:

    - manipulatives appropriate for the task that can be represented in the final copy

    - paper or graphic organizers (such as the Math Four Square from Chapter 10) for drafting solution strategies (at least one per group member)

    - paper or poster paper for creating the final copy (one per group)

    - bold markers in several colors for creating the final copy

3. Have students brainstorm approaches to solving the problem. Encourage them to make rough drawings or notes as they are making sense of the task and what is required to represent and solve it.

4. After brainstorming, have students pursue an approach or representation for solving the problem. As part of their draft, they should keep work associated with all attempts they make at solving the task, including false starts, dead ends, and mistakes. (It can help to ask students to work in pen or marker on their draft so that they cannot erase their work.) As students prepare their draft, encourage them to explain and critique their own arguments with their group mates.

5. Have students discuss which parts of the draft should be transferred to their final copy, in what order, and with what organization. In addition, students should consider what they can add to the work to make their mathematical thinking as clear and complete as possible. After this discussion, students should create the final copy.

6. Monitor students as they work, ask questions that facilitate the work on their drafts, and help them decide what to include in their final copies.

7. Select students to present their work, considering which approaches you can highlight to address the targeted mathematical concepts. Also, determine the sequence in which students will present their work. Aim for a sequence that promotes comparisons of and connections among the representations and approaches that students share. Let selected students know you will ask them to share during the Discuss phase, and give them an opportunity to rehearse what they will say about their work.

Solution Draft and Final Copy in math offers many of the same benefits as it does in other subject areas, such as an opportunity to identify and correct errors and to revise work so it is communicated in a clearer way. However, this technique is unique in math in that it provides a format for students to generate and compare different approaches and representations that reveal mathematical structures, regularities, and connections, promoting stronger math discourse during the Explore phase.

SUPPORTS THAT HELP WITH SOLUTION DRAFT AND FINAL COPY

As students get started and make progress with Solution Draft and Final Copy, they may need support with several aspects of the technique. The following can help them have success with Solution Draft and Final Copy:

Sample drafts. Opportunities to see examples of drafts that are not 100% correct may help students who are still learning that it's okay to make mistakes. You can provide sample drafts that show false starts, dead ends, or mistakes for students to examine and discuss. You can create these samples yourself or use work from volunteer students in your class.

Whole-class final copy. When you first introduce Solution Draft and Final Copy, it may be helpful to have the whole class work together to create a final copy based on a draft. By creating the final copy together, you can model the kind of thinking you hope students will engage in when working on their final copies without your help.

THINK ABOUT IT

To what extent do your students persevere when they struggle with false starts, dead ends, or mistakes in their work? If you were to create a sample draft designed to help them move past initial struggles, what kind of work would you include, and what kind of questions would you ask your students in order to shape the discussion?

Graphic organizer. Students may struggle with organizing their mathematical thinking on the final copy. A graphic organizer can be used to support the draft and to present the final copy. For example, a Math Four Square (Chapter 10) can provide a structure for students to brainstorm and record their thinking in a clear and understandable way for presentation.

Opportunity to rehearse. Students selected to present final copies to the whole class during the Discuss phase may not be prepared to verbally explain their work without practice. It's important to give these students time to rehearse ahead of their presentation so they can articulate their ideas clearly and decide which portions of the explanation will be covered by each group member. This opportunity is always important for emergent math communicators.

Supports for academic language. While creating and rehearsing to present the final copy, students, particularly emergent multilingual learners and emergent math communicators, may benefit from supports that develop their academic language and allow for multiple modes of communication. For example, a math word bank or sentence starters tailored to the task can support students in creating and sharing their final copy.

SIGNS OF SUCCESS

- Students try multiple approaches on their drafts, including approaches that are out of their comfort zones.

- Students discuss their successes and mistakes with their groups before deciding what to include in the final copy.

- All students in the group participate meaningfully in deciding which ideas to include in the final copy and how those will be represented to communicate them clearly.

CAUTION SIGNALS

- Students erase mistakes and false starts on their drafts. (Remind students that mistakes are part of the process of doing math, and perhaps share a draft with a mistake and highlight how much you can learn from that mistake.)

- Final copies reproduce the work of each student's draft, rather than purposefully selecting the work that best represents their collective thinking. (Ask students to discuss which solution best captures their group's thinking and why, and ask them to include only information relevant to that solution in their final copy.)

IMPROVING AND ADAPTING SOLUTION DRAFT AND FINAL COPY

The following ideas will support you in going deeper with and extending this technique.

Not-quite-final copies. If your students are just learning to record their work, they may not initially be prepared to create a stand-alone final copy. In this case, you may accept individual words, invented spellings, pictures, symbols, and other modes of communicating their ideas in the final copy. As your students develop more proficiency in recording their ideas, raise the expectations for completeness and clarity in the final copy until students are able to produce a stand-alone math product.

Draft presentations. As students learn the Solution Draft and Final Copy technique, it may also be helpful to have them present both their final copy and their draft to the whole class during the Discuss phase. You can ask students to share how and why they made specific math choices about what from their draft to include on the final copy. When having students present both the Solution Draft and Final Copy, it is still important to sequence student presentations so that the important concepts come out in an order that supports the goals for the lesson.

Gallery walk. One effective method for sharing multiple final copies is a gallery walk. This format highlights the need to create a final copy that can stand alone to clearly communicate the group's thinking and solution. Small groups prepare their final copies on poster paper and display them around the room. Each group then circulates throughout the room, examining each poster, and recording questions or ideas they have for each group on sticky notes. After the gallery walk, students may revise their final copy based on this feedback. Or you may decide to further explore a mathematical idea highlighted by the feedback.

Half-and-half gallery walk. You might also consider implementing a half-and-half gallery walk. Have half of the students in each group stay at their poster to present their work and answer questions, while the other half circulates. Then the students exchange places for a second round of the gallery walk.

EXAMINE PRACTICE

Read the following vignette from Ms. Manning, who used Solution Draft and Final Copy in the Explore phase. Consider students' approaches observed during this lesson. How does the Solution Draft and Final Copy technique support Ms. Manning in sequencing student presentations to highlight the important math content of the lesson?

Solution Draft and Final Copy in Ms. Manning's Fifth-Grade Classroom

Planning the Lesson

My goal for this lesson was for students to collaboratively solve real-world problems involving fractions using the four-step problem-solving model. My students are comfortable with the four-step model, which consists of (1) understand, (2) plan, (3) solve, and (4) check. My discourse goals touched on all dimensions of the Matrix: I wanted students to listen to their classmates' ideas, ask clarifying questions, and explain their thinking and reasoning. I also wanted students to use multiple modes of communication to represent their ideas.

The lesson came from our district's curriculum. It asked students to solve a variety of story problems with fractions. Some problems required students to divide two whole numbers, resulting in a fraction. Other problems had a unit fraction as the divisor. I anticipated that students would struggle to use flexible strategies when presented with a mixed set of problems, even though we have worked with each type of problem in isolation. I expected students to listen to each group member's thinking in order to establish shared solution strategies and to question each other to clarify understanding.

I planned for students to use the Solution Draft and Final Copy technique in the Explore phase. This year, my students have not used this technique in math. We use drafts and final copies as part of our writing lessons all the time. I thought their experience with this practice in literacy would help.

(continued)

EXAMINE PRACTICE (continued)

I wanted students to first collectively record their solutions on their draft. I planned to share one paper among the four students and ask them to use pens of different colors to ensure all group members participated equitably. This paper included a modified Math Four Square to represent the steps in our four-step model. Students would get a second paper later for their final copies. I told them they needed to focus on making their mathematical thinking and reasoning visible to others who might view their final copy.

Enacting the Lesson

I started the lesson with my 33 students sitting on the carpet. I reviewed the learning objective displayed on the board and launched the lesson by modeling what we do in the four-step model and reminding students what each step requires. Next, we moved on to the Explore phase and started work on the following problem:

> Jordan needs to fill a bucket with 6 pounds of rocks for their garden.
>
> They are using a scoop to fill the bucket with rocks.
>
> If each scoop holds $\frac{1}{8}$ of a pound, how many scoops will they need?

Most groups began by identifying the important pieces of information in the problem and writing them in the *understand* quadrant of their drafts. For example, one student listed the number of pounds needed and the amount of rocks in each scoop. At least two groups recorded the question they had to answer: "How many scoops are needed?" I was glad to see that many groups wrote the equation $6 \div \frac{1}{8} = s$, using s for the solution, in the *plan* quadrant of their drafts and final copies. Their work showed me they understood the division they would need to carry out to solve the problem. Most groups also recorded their use of a visual model as a strategy.

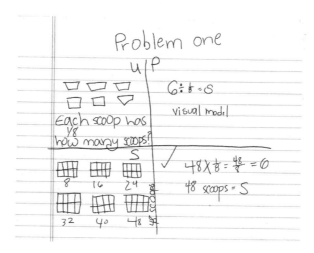

The *solve* quadrant of students' drafts was the most interesting. Several groups began by drawing six rectangles and dividing each rectangle into eight pieces. One group wrote 8 above each rectangle, indicating that the rectangle had 8 pieces. They recorded the answer "48 scoops." Another group wrote a running total above each rectangle: 8, 16, 24, 32, 40, 48. As I walked around monitoring the work, I also saw one group that wrote $\frac{1}{8}$ for each part and concluded they needed $\frac{6}{8}$. I asked them to explain what Jordan was trying to do in the problem situation. They realized they were not counting the number of scoops, and they needed to find out how many $\frac{1}{8}$-pound scoops were in the 6 pounds. When I asked them how many scoops, they said 8. I further probed, "8 scoops in what?" They explained 8 scoops was for 1 pound, and I let them continue discussing and reasoning on their own. I saw another group in which one student had the same misconception, but I decided not to intervene because I heard the group disagreeing and examining their reasoning together.

Several groups moved on to the second problem:

> Dr. Wright is hosting a pizza party for her graduate school class of 10 students.
>
> If 8 pizzas are purchased, how much pizza will each student receive?

(continued)

EXAMINE PRACTICE (continued)

This time, the drafts were really showing students' solutions and work. I saw circular fraction models and rectangular fraction models that made it into students' final copies. Most students wrote accurate equations. I also monitored to make sure my emergent multilingual learners were participating. I approached one group where one student was clearly quiet and reluctant to speak up. I asked the student to tell me the equation for the problem. I offered the sentence starter "My equation to this problem was …" and the student was able to answer. Then I suggested that we think about other sentence starters the group could use when needed. We generated a few possibilities, which helped get the students more equitably engaged. When most groups had a solution to at least one problem, I asked the class to move on to their final copies.

Reflecting on the Explore Phase

For the most part, I think the lesson unfolded as I expected and met my math goals, except that some groups did not complete their final copy. Students used the draft as a way to make sense of the problems and decide on a solution method for each type of problem. Some groups had misconceptions about how the $\frac{1}{8}$ and the 6 related in the context of the first problem, but they were able to model the problem correctly. Students were also able to explain their strategies effectively at the end of the lesson. In a few instances, I saw groups make mistakes, but they self-corrected before I needed to step in with probing questions.

The use of Solution Draft and Final Copy, together with the modified Math Four Square, allowed my students to focus their thinking. They engaged in productive and collaborative math dialogue about the fraction division problems and how to solve them. Giving students one piece of paper to share encouraged them to work together rather than independently. Even students who need more practice with social cues in group settings were able to successfully collaborate when given some coaching and support. Overall, I would say the use of the draft allowed student groups to engage in productive math dialogue around fraction division story problems with whole number or fraction divisors. Both the draft and the final copy gave them practice with representing and explaining their ideas in ways that others could understand.

Examining Ms. Manning's Explore Phase

The purposeful use of discourse techniques during the Explore phase of this lesson supports the students in making their mathematical arguments explicit. Ms. Manning scaffolded students' drafts by providing them with a structure and got students to work together by making sure they shared one draft that was later organized into their final copies. With several different representations available for discussion, Ms. Manning was ready to engage students in sharing and critiquing their mathematical reasoning, helping students make sense of story problems with fractions.

DISCUSS WITH COLLEAGUES

1 What challenges might your students face when working on creating their drafts? What mathematical opportunities might be available to students as they transition from the draft to the final copy?

2 What supports could you implement during their work on drafts that would strengthen your students' skills in representing and explaining their mathematical thinking on the final copy?

CONNECT TO YOUR PRACTICE

Choose a math problem that students can explore using the Solution Draft and Final Copy technique. List the approaches you expect students to use.

☐ What manipulatives can you provide students to support these approaches?

☐ How do these approaches highlight the targeted mathematical concepts?

☐ What common mistakes do you expect to see?

☐ How might you sequence the presentation of these approaches (and possibly mistakes) during the Discuss phase to address key mathematical ideas?

Now try the Solution Draft and Final Copy technique with your students.

NOTES

_____

_____

_____

KEY TAKEAWAYS ABOUT THE EXPLORE PHASE

Part IV shared four techniques and vignettes that engaged students with the math journey of the lesson: Think-Pair-Rehearse-Share, Math Four Square, Talk Triangle, and Solution Draft and Final Copy. These techniques in action remind us that the Explore phase is when most of the student-to-student discourse takes place and all students should participate meaningfully and equitably in this phase. Here are the main takeaways from these chapters:

- Actively engage throughout the Explore phase, and ensure that all your students, particularly emergent multilingual learners, are participating and making sense of the math.

- Purposefully support your students in using questioning, listening, explaining, and different modes of communication with one another during this phase.

- Prepare in advance for what to do when students have incorrect solutions or unexpected approaches—take into account their productive struggle and the role you might want these solutions or approaches to play in the Discuss phase.

- Remember that time is always a constraint; plan clearly and manage how the Explore phase unfolds to keep the class moving toward your goals.

- Always consider the balance between quantity and quality of work carried out in the Explore phase to make sure your students are ready for a successful Discuss phase.

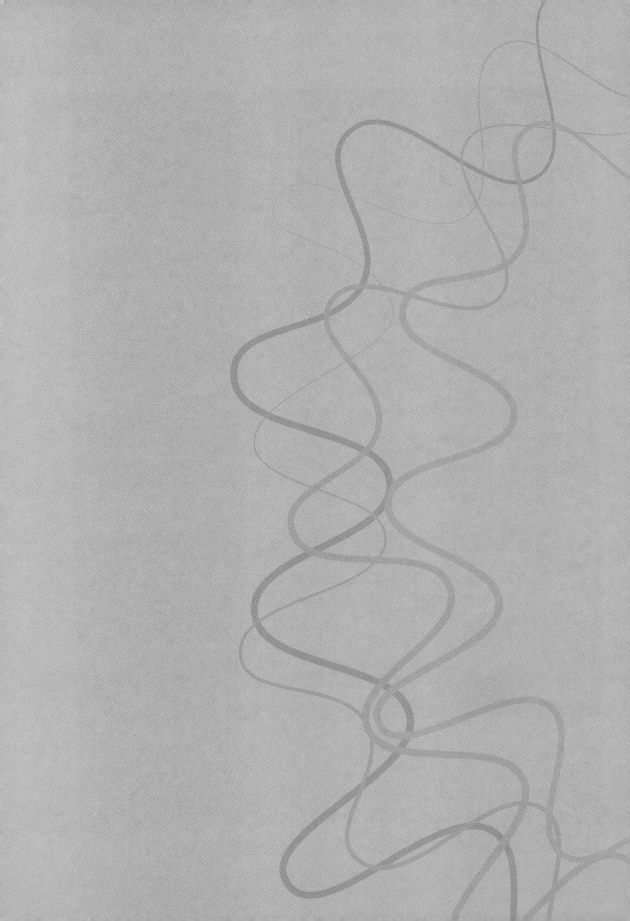

Talk Techniques for the Discuss Phase

Up to this point, your students have been exploring the mathematical terrain, seeing new sights, and maybe taking some wrong turns along the way. They are now in the home stretch; their destination—understanding the math goal—is in sight. How do you help them get there?

Orchestrating a successful whole-group, student-centered discussion is an art. It requires a fine balance of giving students ownership of the mathematical work and the discussions about that work, while still providing scaffolds that guide those discussions in meaningful ways toward the targeted learning goals of the lesson. Part V presents four talk techniques you can use during the Discuss phase and illustrates their use in real classroom settings:

- Math Talk Chain (Chapter 13)
- All Talk Math (Chapter 14)
- Probing and Pressing Math Questions (Chapter 15)
- Math Learning Summary (Chapter 16)

13

Math Talk Chain

In both math as well as reading and writing, students can be very enthusiastic about sharing with the class when they have a great idea. However, it's less common for students to have this same enthusiasm for listening to others and making connections among different ideas. The Math Talk Chain technique provides a structure that requires students to listen carefully to their peers' mathematical ideas and consider connections before sharing their own thinking.

WHAT IS MATH TALK CHAIN?

Math Talk Chain: a discussion format in which students listen to and acknowledge what the previous contributor has said before explaining their own ideas to engage in a mathematically connected conversation

The Math Talk Chain is a discussion format in which every student who participates has to first restate what was previously said, and then add their own ideas while connecting them to the prior one. For example, after listening to a peer's mathematical thinking, a student may respond, "I heard you say . . . . I also think . . . ." This format requires students to listen to and acknowledge what others are saying before explaining their own ideas to support making mathematical connections.

The Math Talk Chain technique builds on experiences your students may have already had with restating and asks students to take the additional step of sharing a new idea, critique, or question that connects to a previously shared idea. Though it may feel somewhat unnatural, the Math Talk Chain serves as a scaffold to help students move toward responsive discourse in which listening is expected and students' contributions are connected and relevant to the conversation, furthering their mathematical understanding of the conversation.

WHY MIGHT YOU USE MATH TALK CHAIN?

When waiting for their turn to contribute to a discussion, students often wave a hand in the air and focus on what they want to share without listening carefully to each other's mathematical ideas or thinking about how their contribution fits in. Math Talk Chain promotes these skills of listening and making connections while also giving students more responsibility for the discussion.

Purposes of Math Talk Chain

- Engage students in listening to and understanding their peers' ideas
- Support students in considering their solution method in relation to other methods and articulating mathematical connections among them
- Encourage students to compare and contrast mathematical arguments and results
- Provide structures and opportunities for students to take ownership of and responsibility for the mathematical discussions

Accomplishing these purposes during the Discuss phase helps students make meaning of the mathematical work they did during the Explore phase and clear up any lingering misconceptions. It also develops students' abilities to engage in probing and responsive discourse.

GETTING STARTED WITH MATH TALK CHAIN

Each turn of a Math Talk Chain consists of two basic parts: restating what the previous speaker said and making another statement that connects to what the previous speaker said. Consider the following fourth-grade division story problem:

Taylor and Selena are making bouquets of wildflowers to sell at their school fundraiser. Taylor picked daisies and made bouquets of 7 flowers. Selena picked sunflowers and made bouquets of 4 flowers. If each girl picked 125 flowers and made as many bouquets as possible, who had the most flowers left over?

A Math Talk Chain for this problem might start something like this:

SCENARIO 13-1

A student presenter, Alex, explains that he divided 125 by 7 to get 17 full bouquets of daisies and 125 by 4 to get 31 full bouquets of sunflowers and that Selena had the most bouquets.

Kara: I heard Alex say Selena had the most bouquets. I agree and disagree. I agree with the number of bouquets, but I think that the question asked who had the most flowers left over. Taylor had the most left over.

Jason: Kara said Taylor had the most left over. I agree and I want to add on to that. Taylor had 6 daisies left over and Selena had 1 sunflower left over.

Angelica: Jason said Taylor had 6 daisies left over and Selena had 1 sunflower left over. My question about that idea is how did Jason know how much was left over?

Miguel: Angelica asked how Jason knew what each girl had left over. I was confused about Taylor, but I knew Selena had one left over because 4 times 30 is 120, and 5 is one more than 4, so Selena has 1 more bouquet and 1 left over.

Alex: Miguel said he was confused about Taylor, and I now see what the question is asking. The number of bouquets for Taylor is 17, and when I calculated 17 multiplied by 7, I got 119. Because Taylor had 125 flowers, there were 6 left over.

In this example, students use the Math Talk Chain structure to resolve a misunderstanding about what the question was asking, share their results and approaches, and bring up aspects of the problem they were still unsure about. Through the Math Talk Chain, students cleared up several mathematical issues and took responsibility for the mathematical discussion of the group. Ideally, you want to continue the Math Talk Chain through enough turns for students to explain and justify their approaches with more conceptual depth, make connections among these approaches, and come to a resolution and understanding about the final result.

To implement the Math Talk Chain technique, use the following steps:

1. Begin with a prompt or a question, and select a student to respond to it.
2. Ask another student to start the chain by first restating an idea shared by the prior student and then making their own contribution. Students may contribute in a variety of ways:
   - agreeing or disagreeing and explaining why
   - adding on to what was shared
   - asking a question about what was shared
   - sharing a different approach
3. Have another student repeat the same process: Restate what the prior student said, and make a new contribution. You can select the next student in a variety of ways, based on your students' needs. You might call on a volunteer if your class is highly engaged, select a student yourself to ensure all students have a chance to speak, or have the first student call on the next student if your class is ready to take more ownership of the mathematical discussion.
4. Ask additional students to continue the Math Talk Chain, following these general rules:
   - Contributions should connect with what was said immediately before each speaker's turn.
   - Students may ask questions or change the direction of the conversation.
   - If students don't catch what the previous student said, they may ask the previous student to repeat.
   - Student contributions may include various modes of communication to support their verbal explanations (e.g., manipulatives, pictures, written work).
   - If someone "breaks the chain" or the conversation gets off track, the teacher, or even a student, can redirect the Math Talk Chain.
5. Continue the chain for as long as needed to bring out the important mathematical ideas, discuss how those ideas connect to one another, and resolve any misconceptions that surface during the Explore or Discuss phase.

THINK ABOUT IT

How could you support students in incorporating nonverbal modes of communication into the Math Talk Chain?

SUPPORTS THAT HELP WITH MATH TALK CHAIN

When you first introduce Math Talk Chain to your class, students may find the technique unnatural and struggle with following the strict format. Even as the class gains familiarity with the technique, some students, especially emergent communicators, may benefit from continued support. The following ideas can help your students get started and experience continued success with Math Talk Chain:

Sentence starters. Students may be unsure how to restate their peers' ideas and connect their own, and sentence starters can serve as an essential scaffold. They are particularly helpful when you first introduce your class to the technique and as a continued support for emergent communicators. Here are some sentence starters you might use:

- [Name] said that . . . . I (agree/disagree) with it because . . . .
- [Name] said that . . . . I agree and disagree. I agree that . . ., but I think that . . . .
- [Name] said that . . . . I want to add to what you said. My idea is . . . .
- I understand [name] said . . . . My idea is different. Our ideas are different because . . . .
- I heard [name] say . . . . My question about that idea is . . . .

Modeling expected responses. Use sentence starters to model how students might participate in the Math Talk Chain technique. You may need to help students, especially young learners, form their responses with the sentence starters at first, saying the sentence starter with each student who speaks until they begin using the sentence starters themselves.

Link goals. Set goals for the number of "links" (that is, the number of students who contribute) to be completed during a Math Talk Chain to create a fun challenge. As students improve with the Math Talk Chain, you can increase the goal to build stamina with deeper and more connected conversations. Using actual links (paper, plastic) to create a chain, adding a link for each student who contributes, or other means of tracking how many students have added to the mathematical discussion can help motivate students to reach the goal.

Math Talk Chain monitor. Have a student helper be the Math Talk Chain monitor. If a student breaks the chain, the monitor can ring a bell to draw attention to the fact that the participant did not follow the Math Talk Chain rules.

Yarn ball. Use a ball of yarn to represent the flow of the conversation and motivate students to get involved. One person holds the ball of yarn and speaks. After speaking, that student chooses another student volunteer to speak. While still holding the end of the yarn, the student throws the yarn ball to the next speaker, creating an effective link between those speakers and reminding the next speaker to restate what the previous student said. This process continues throughout the discussion. Setting restrictions, such as holding the yarn only once or twice, can encourage even more students to participate.

SIGNS OF SUCCESS

- Students restate their peers' mathematical contributions accurately, even if they disagree with what was shared.

- Students' contributions meaningfully connect to the prior student's mathematical ideas.

- The Math Talk Chain continues for many turns, allowing the majority of students to share their thinking and deepen the conversation.

CAUTION SIGNALS

- Students don't remember what the prior person said, or they restate the prior student's contribution incorrectly. (Direct students to ask the prior person to repeat their contribution or whether they restated what was said correctly.)

- Students' contributions do not add to the mathematical reasoning of the discussion (e.g., "I agree with her because that's the answer I got."), possibly resulting in the Math Talk Chain ending prematurely. (Ask students to add on to weak contributions with a deeper explanation, a new approach, a justification, or a question before continuing to the next student.)

IMPROVING AND ADAPTING MATH TALK CHAIN

Once you are comfortable with the basic steps of the Math Talk Chain, there are a few recommendations for how to better prepare for and use this technique with students, including ideas for adaptation.

Small groups. It may be helpful to introduce the Math Talk Chain technique in small groups. This structure gives each student a chance to practice making contributions to the Math Talk Chain without the pressure of speaking in front of the whole class. Once students have gained some familiarity with the Math Talk Chain in their small groups, you can transition to using the technique in a whole-class format.

Focus on structure. As students are getting used to the Math Talk Chain, allow them to make contributions that fulfill the basic structure of the technique, restating what was said and sharing a new idea or question, even if their contributions are not particularly deep or connected to what was shared. As students gain comfort with the Math Talk Chain, push them to make meaningful mathematical connections to their peers' reasoning or to ask questions that spark deeper mathematical insight.

Avoid one-on-one talk. Although students are allowed to ask clarifying questions in the Math Talk Chain structure, it is important that the discussion not become a one-on-one conversation between two students. If you notice that the Math Talk Chain has become a pair speaking back and forth, you can ask that the question be posed to the whole group, call on other students, or restart the Math Talk Chain.

Evolve into a whole-group discussion. Keep in mind that Math Talk Chain is a step along the way to helping students learn how to engage in responsive discourse. It's a scaffold to help them take more responsibility for the mathematical discussion. During the Discuss phase, you may begin by using Math Talk Chain, but then let the conversation evolve into a natural whole-group discussion. Let students know they no longer have to follow the Math Talk Chain rules, but they do need to continue to listen to and address one another's ideas. Remember, the objective is to have responsive discussions in which students share and critique mathematical arguments and connect representations.

EXAMINE PRACTICE

Ms. LaFuente's first-grade students are working on math story problems. As you read this vignette, ask yourself: How did Ms. LaFuente's interventions in the Math Talk Chain affect students' math discourse and learning? Consider what strategies this teacher used and which additional strategies could keep the Math Talk Chain productive.

Math Talk Chain in Ms. LaFuente's First-Grade Classroom

Planning the Lesson

Twenty-two of my 26 years in teaching have been in first grade. And every time I give my first graders a story problem, they tend to think about adding first. In this lesson, I wanted students to recognize that today's task required finding the difference between the numbers in the problem, not adding them. Then, students could use any strategy for subtraction, like count back, take away, think addition, or show on a number line. To support their attention to the problem, I planned to use Math Bet Lines in the Launch phase. And to have several solution strategies presented, I used Solution Draft and Final Copy during the Explore phase. The final copies were to become part of our discussion, and I planned to use the Math Talk Chain in the Discuss phase, which is my focus of this story.

I had several discourse goals related to the Matrix. I wanted my students to ask each other questions to clarify ideas or solution methods. I also wanted them to volunteer their own thinking for their solution methods as part of their explanations. Finally, I wanted my students to listen to their peers and make connections among these peers' ideas and their own. I thought the Math Talk Chain technique would be great for this last purpose and for releasing some of the discourse responsibilities to my students.

(continued)

EXAMINE PRACTICE (continued)

Enacting the Lesson

When my 17 students were on the carpet in the front of the room, I displayed my learning goal for them: "I can solve addition and subtraction problems in a variety of ways." I launched the lesson using the Math Bet Lines technique, showing one line of the problem at a time.

> Lily had 8 rocks in her collection.
>
> Joshua had 14 rocks in his.
>
> How many more rocks did Joshua have than Lily?

During the Explore phase, students worked with their assigned partners using white boards to solve the problem. Toward the end of the Explore phase, I selected three groups to present their final copies to the whole group.

When we started the discussion, I explained we would engage in a Math Talk Chain after each one of the shared solution strategies. I pointed students to the sentence starters that were on the board:

_____ said that _____

I agree with _____ because _____

I disagree with _____ because _____

I want to add that _____

The first student pair shared that they had used a number line. They explained how they counted up from 8 to 14 to determine that 14 is 6 more than 8.

14 is 6 more then 8

The Math Talk Chain that followed was not very long, and I had to help students keep it going, but I was happy the students were able to hear and correct a silly mistake without my help. The chain here is how I remember it. Samantha started it when she restated the group's solution.

Samantha: So Lily had 8 and Joshua had 14, and as you see 14 is 6 more than 8. In the sentence it says 14 is more than 8. 14 is 6 more than 8.

Carlos: I heard you say 14 is more than 8, so 6 is more than 8. I agree because we had 6 for the answer.

Zaire: I heard Carlos say I agree, but I disagree with one thing you said: 6 is more than 8.

Samantha: No, 14 is more than 8.

Zaire: Yes, I agree that 14 is more than 8. 14 is 6 more than 8. But 6 is not more than 8.

Me (adding to the chain): I hear the correction Zaire is making to what Carlos said—6 is not more than 8—good point, and we can continue.

Diana: I heard Samantha say that they jumped 6 more from 8 and got to the number 14.

Me (prompting Diana): Using what strategy?

(continued)

EXAMINE PRACTICE (continued)

Diana: They jumped 6 more from 8 and got to the number 14 using the number line.

Jackson: I heard you say they jumped 6 and I agree because that is like what I did, like 8 and 6 more. That is 14.

Me: So what is the answer to the problem?

Brad: I think Samantha is saying that Joshua had 6 more rocks.

Me: Very nice. I agree, and let's give this group a hand.

Students continued sharing final copies. The next group had the answer 7. I had not intentionally picked a group that had an incorrect answer, but between me letting them know they would share and them actually sharing, they changed their answer. I chose this group because they had a number line and a picture matching 14 counters and 8 counters. But in their final copy, they actually represented 15 counters. So when they matched the two, their answer was 7. I let them explain, and the Math Talk Chain started.

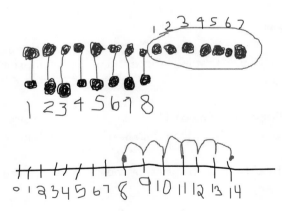

Kevin: I used the connect strategy to match the numbers and find out it was 7. And my partner Aaron used a number line. The difference between 14 and 8 is 7.

Julia: I heard you say that the answer is 7, and I disagree. We got 6.

Kevin: Okay, you say it is wrong. We used the connect strategy, and we had the lines connecting the pairs between 14 and 8. And when you count what is left, that is 7.

Me (to get the conversation going): Let's hold on to this thought and talk about the number line for a little. Did you count back from 14 to 8?

Aaron: I did count back: 14, 13, 12, 11, 10, 9, 8.

Samantha: I heard you say that it was 7, and I disagree, and when you counted back, I think you accidentally counted the 14 with it. You do not count the 14. So when we used a number line, we counted 6 more.

Aaron: I heard you say to not count the 14, but, like, we have to start at the 14. I start on the 14. I have 14, 13, 12, 11, 10, 9, 8.

Samantha: I heard you say 14, 13, but when you start at the 14, you first count the 13. When you do like that, you go to the 8.

Aaron: I heard you say to start at the 13. Okay. 13, 12, 11, 10, 9, 8. That would be 6.

Samantha: Yes, 6. We counted 9, 10, 11, 12, 13, 14, and you did 13, 12, 11, 10, 9, 8. It is 6.

Me (returning the conversation to the matches): I hear you have two ways to count. That is very interesting. Maybe the other side of your representations was not accurate, because the number line seems to be right if we count it correctly. What should we do?

John: Use a different one [strategy] than just small dots.

(continued)

EXAMINE PRACTICE (continued)

Jackson: John said use another way. I think that instead of another way, we should check the small dots.

Me: I heard Jackson say we should check the dots. The dots are super neat. Let's recount them.

At this point, I interrupted the chain because there was a lot going on mathematically with the counting strategies and it was easier just to see that they accidentally had 15 dots in their comparison. We then moved to the final group that had different solutions, and one was an equation to show their thinking. They had 8 + 6 = 14 and they said there was a missing part, like a "p," and that "p" was 6 in their equation, so they knew what needed to add to 8 to get to 14. For this conversation, I wanted to probe a little more and decided not to use the Math Talk Chain. Using an equation was different for most of my kids, and I needed a different format for our conversation. During the Explore phase, I had worked with that group to connect their number line and equation, but I knew the class needed more time to process this idea.

Reflecting on the Discuss Phase

Overall, the class went as expected, and I think I achieved my goals. The two Math Talk Chains brought out some good discussion among the students. I wanted a little more depth, so I ended up adding to the discussions. Perhaps if I had let the chain run longer, they would have made sense of what was shared and resolved any discrepancies more independently. Still, students did well communicating accurately with the class. I think the Math Talk Chains around the first two presentations moved us well toward the last group's presentation of the equation. I thought this group would use subtraction, but instead they thought about the problem as addition and wrote the equation 8 + 6 = 14. Because most groups solved with a number line or matching comparison, discussing this group's work gave the rest of the class an opportunity to consider a solution strategy that they had not used themselves. I'm not confident all my students understood how that group came up with the equation, but I was pleased that the conversation exposed students to equations and reinforced the idea that there are multiple approaches to solving a problem.

Examining Ms. LaFuente's Discuss Phase

By using the Math Talk Chain technique in the presentation of students' solutions, Ms. LaFuente addresses the discourse goals of having students listen to each other and ask clarifying questions. The teacher actively engages with the two Math Talk Chains to guide the conversation in productive ways, supporting students as they address mistakes that emerged in the conversation and increasing the precision of the mathematical argumentation. Making decisions about when to intervene, when to continue the chain, and when to let go of the technique in order to use other formats to increase the quality of the classroom math discourse, Ms. LaFuente orchestrates the discussion toward the key content goals of the lesson.

DISCUSS WITH COLLEAGUES

1   What aspects of the Math Talk Chain might be the most challenging for your students (e.g., listening, explaining their idea, connecting their idea to the previous idea, taking turns)? What supports would help them be successful in these areas?

2   What strategies can you use to ensure that all students in your class are able to contribute meaningfully to the Math Talk Chain?

3   How can you most effectively intervene if your Math Talk Chain gets off track or breaks?

CONNECT TO YOUR PRACTICE

Plan a lesson where students will use the Math Talk Chain technique to discuss their mathematical ideas and make connections among those ideas. Make a list of the mathematical ideas and connections you hope will emerge, and prepare questions that will encourage students to make these connections. Enact the Math Talk Chain with your class, and reflect on the successes and challenges that your class encountered. What might you do differently next time and why?

NOTES

_____

_____

_____

_____

_____

_____

_____

_____

_____

_____

_____

_____

_____

_____

All Talk Math

In many classrooms there are typically a handful of students who consistently volunteer to share their thinking while others are more hesitant to contribute to discussions. Yet we know that all students have mathematical thinking worth sharing. It can be challenging for teachers to help all students feel comfortable having a voice in the discussion and sharing their thinking. And it is often the case that the longer students go without participating in large-group discourse, the harder it is for them to break into it. The All Talk Math technique is designed to give every student an equal opportunity to participate in the discussion and share their own ideas, bringing each of them into the conversation in a safe and productive way.

WHAT IS ALL TALK MATH?

In All Talk Math, the teacher provides a prompt related to a math question or problem and then all students take turns sharing a brief idea related to the prompt, giving every student the opportunity and support they need to participate. Students can choose to add a new idea or repeat someone else's answer in their own words—the important part is that every single student gets to say something to the whole group that is substantive and related to the prompt. Because you want all students to participate, answers to the prompt have to be brief—in fact, very brief—for the round of All Talk Math to go quickly. Thus, All Talk Math is a quick and versatile technique that can be used along with various supports like question prompts and sentence starters.

All Talk Math: a technique in which all students take turns sharing a brief idea related to the math prompt

WHY MIGHT YOU USE ALL TALK MATH?

The main purpose of the All Talk Math technique is to allow all students to participate and have a voice in the discussion. Students may share a strategy for solving a problem, what they found most challenging, or even their answer to the problem—depending on the prompt.

There are many purposes for using All Talk Math during the Discuss phase of the lesson. For instance, you can use the technique at the beginning of the discussion to allow students to share their initial impressions of the problem (e.g., asking what seemed challenging or easy). This initial use of All Talk Math serves as an invitation to all students to join the larger conversation. You can engage students in All Talk Math in the middle of the discussion to allow them to share a strategy they used for solving the problem or their answer. In this case, you get a quick read of where all your students are and you can recalibrate the discussion. You can also use All Talk Math at the end of the discussion to wrap up the task by having students share what they learned or how their new work relates to previous mathematical work.

Purposes of All Talk Math

- Ensure participation from all students, giving them an opportunity to share a mathematical idea with the whole class
- Provide a safe math discourse community where all students, including emergent multilingual learners, feel comfortable and confident sharing their thinking
- Gather evidence quickly about where students are in their mathematical thinking
- Start or summarize a mathematical discussion

GETTING STARTED WITH ALL TALK MATH

The All Talk Math technique can be used in a variety of ways and is a step toward helping all students meaningfully participate in whole-group discussions. When implementing the All Talk Math technique, use the following steps:

1. Provide a question or a prompt that all students can address and clear guidance about what they should share. Questions or prompts should highlight the mathematical features of the math problem, like so:
    *   What parts of this problem were challenging?
    *   How is this problem different from the problems we were working on yesterday?
    *   What strategy did you use to solve this problem?
    *   What type of representation helped you solve this problem?
2. Model one or two responses to support students' full understanding of what they are expected to share. This can help prevent students from sharing too much, causing the All Talk Math to last longer than you planned. Be specific in your guidance about whether students can repeat an idea that was already said.
3. Indicate the order in which students will contribute to ensure a smooth transition from student to student. One way to do this is to use the order in which students are seated.
4. Give students brief quiet time to think about how they will respond. They may want to review work they completed during the Explore phase or write down ideas.
5. Call on the first student to begin All Talk Math by sharing their response. Then move on to the next student, and so forth. Ensure students take turns sharing their ideas quickly without having to be called on.
6. Allow students to repeat ideas that were previously shared if that is what they were also thinking. They should repeat the idea in their own words rather than just say that they had the same idea as another student.

The more practice students have with this technique, the more comfortable they will become sharing their ideas with the whole class.

THINK ABOUT IT

How can you make sure your emergent multilingual learners are ready to participate in All Talk Math? What scaffolds can you use?

SUPPORTS THAT HELP WITH ALL TALK MATH

For students to feel comfortable and confident taking risks when sharing their thinking, offering substantial support is critical. The following are some supports you can try.

Purposeful ordering. The goal for All Talk Math is for all students to participate in the discussion, and some students may benefit from additional support. One thing you can do is make purposeful decisions about the order in which students share. For example, with some advance notice and preparation, have those who may be struggling respond early in All Talk Math, offering them an opportunity to share an idea before other students share the same idea. You can also allow students to skip their turn and share their response at the end of All Talk Math if they need more time to think. Reminding students they can repeat an idea can also make it easier for some of them to participate.

Sentence starters. Offer students sentence starters they can use when contributing to All Talk Math. These starters can help students with the structure of the technique and the types of responses you are expecting. They can also prevent the discussion from lasting longer than expected.

Preview during Explore phase. Another way to support students is to highlight or preview certain ideas that they may like to share during All Talk Math. Based on your interactions with students and monitoring of their work in the Explore phase, you can give them ideas of what they can share during the upcoming All Talk Math and encourage them to rehearse. Similarly, emergent multilingual learners may benefit from receiving the prompt and sentence starters in advance to give them time to consider their response before All Talk Math begins.

SIGNS OF SUCCESS

- Students quickly share their ideas without having to be reminded of the question or prompt, or whose turn it is.

- Students attend to mathematical aspects of the question or prompt as appropriate.

- All students comfortably share their ideas with the whole class.

CAUTION SIGNALS

- The majority of students share ideas that are irrelevant to the mathematical aspects of the question or prompt. (Pause All Talk Math to introduce a new sentence frame that may help the remaining students.)

- All Talk Math is taking up too much time. (Model the type of brief response you are expecting.)

IMPROVING AND ADAPTING ALL TALK MATH

All Talk Math is a versatile technique that can be used with lots of changes and adaptations. The overall goal is to get all students engaged and participating in whole-group conversations, establishing a classroom community where all students feel safe sharing their mathematical thinking regularly.

Build on more discussion. You may consider continuing the whole-group discussion after All Talk Math to highlight specific student responses. For example, you could ask students to respond to a specific student who shared something interesting or two students who shared similar or different ideas.

Start with a friend. All Talk Math can be used along with other techniques that give students the opportunity to support each other. For example, you can begin with Think-Pair-Rehearse-Share (Chapter 9), with each pair of students contributing an idea. Another well-known technique that may complement All Talk Math is Turn and Talk, which can be used to help students develop a response to the question or prompt before sharing.

Use in the Launch or Explore phase. The All Talk Math technique can be used in the Launch or Explore phase of the lesson. In the Launch phase, for example, you may use it to discuss vocabulary in an assigned problem and to help students recall important prior knowledge. In the Explore phase, you may ask small groups to do All Talk Math before working to solve a problem as a way to keep any single student from dominating the group conversation.

EXAMINE PRACTICE

Ms. Abdal uses All Talk Math in the Discuss phase to hear her students' explanations and gauge their understanding of how to compare numbers using the concept of place value. Read the vignette below and ask yourself what Ms. Abdal did to ensure students' responses stayed aligned with the prompt and mathematical goals of the lesson.

(continued)

EXAMINE PRACTICE (continued)

All Talk Math in Ms. Abdal's Second-Grade Classroom

Planning the Lesson

I am a second-grade teacher and have been teaching for 13 years. For this story, I share a lesson where my mathematical goal was to have students compare numbers and use their understanding of place value to support their thinking. I wanted students to use base ten to represent numbers and help them with their mathematical argumentation. My discourse goals were for students to listen and build on each other's ideas about the meaning of place value. I also wanted students to work with a partner to construct their mathematical arguments. I planned to teach a lesson from my district's math instructional materials. I would use Task Think-Aloud in the Launch phase to model how to compare numbers and explain my thinking. Students would work in pairs during the Explore phase. Then I planned to use All Talk Math during the Discuss phase to hear from all of my students in a safe, equitable environment for them.

Enacting the Lesson

My 19 students were working in pairs. I gave them a sheet with several comparison problems and they each selected two problems to complete, for a total of four problems per pair. They worked together to determine if the correct symbol was less than, equal, or greater than for each problem. The partners worked very well together as they compared the numbers they chose.

When we came back to the carpet for the Discuss phase, I had been pretty happy with my students' work. They were for the most part comparing the numbers correctly, although they were sometimes reading 521 < 612 as "612 is bigger than 521." I stopped them during the Explore phase to go over this issue. In most cases, students self-corrected. When we got together to discuss, I asked only one pair to share: Tamecia and Luana. I suggested that they focus on place value and using base ten to compare numbers.

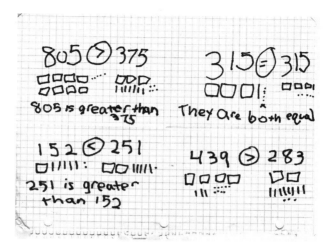

Tamecia chose to talk about 315 and 315. She determined they were equal and showed the numbers in expanded form with base ten blocks. Luana asked her to explain why they were equal, and Tamecia concluded: Both have 3 hundreds, 1 ten, and 5 ones. At that point, I moved to All Talk Math. I had students make a circle and I gave them the following prompt:

> *Using what you know about place value, how can you compare two numbers?*

I reminded students that they could share a new idea or restate or add on to a previously shared idea during All Talk Math. I reiterated the rules: You must listen to each other and stick to the topic; try your best to share your own thinking very directly and briefly. I then picked a student to start, and we followed the circle in the order they were sitting. It went like this:

S1: You can see how much you have to add to get to the other. What's the difference?

S2: You can add to one of them to see how much that makes.

S3: Look at the hundreds, tens, and ones to see which is bigger. You should start with hundreds.

(continued)

EXAMINE PRACTICE (continued)

S4: In place value, there is hundreds, tens, and ones. That makes the numbers you compare.

S5: You can add the numbers and see what they make.

Me: Remember, the question we are answering is: Using what you know about place value, how can you compare two numbers?

S6: You see hundreds, then tens, then ones. If one has more hundreds than the other, it's bigger. If it is the same, you go to tens.

S7: To compare, if it has hundreds, tens, and ones, you can look at the hundreds, then the tens, then the ones.

S8: Place value has to be the most. You start with the largest.

S9: Place value has numbers, and that is what we compare.

Me: Again, we are answering: How can you compare two numbers using place value?

S10: If it's comparing 697 and 679, it's probably trying to trick you. Ones don't matter unless the numbers before it are the same.

S11: Look at the hundreds then tens to see what's bigger. Then the ones.

S12: Look at ones, then tens, then hundreds to see what's bigger.

S13: Compare by looking at the hundreds to see the amount. Then look at the other hundreds. If they're the same, look at the tens. If they're the same, look at the ones.

S14: Place value has value where hundreds are, and tens, and ones. You compare those values.

S15: Place value—you can compare two numbers by looking at the hundreds. If there was 3 hundreds and the other is 1 hundred, you would know 3 is bigger than 1.

S16: In place value there's ones, tens, hundreds, thousands, ten thousands, and goes on and on and on. But when comparing, you start with the largest.

S17: Numbers in place value can go on and on.

Me: How does that help you compare?

S17: It helps me compare numbers by … (silence)

Me: We can come back if you want. The last one to go is the hardest because everyone has shared.

S18: First look at the big one—I don't know what to say.

Me: That's okay. I want to go back to S1, where we started. Can you please repeat what you said?

S1: I said you can use the difference between the numbers.

Me: Can you say more about that?

We ended All Talk Math to examine the issue about finding the difference between the numbers as a way to compare them.

Reflecting on the Discuss Phase

After listening to the All Talk Math responses, I was able to better understand where students were in their thinking. It exposed some students' misunderstandings as well. This was good, although it is always a little surprising when you realize some students did not think about the problem as you expected. A couple of students started talking about adding

(continued)

EXAMINE PRACTICE (continued)

the two numbers. I still have to work to make sense of how they came to that idea to share.

I have one student who is brand new to the United States. This student got here only two days ago. I had the student work with a partner and gave them base ten blocks to show the numbers. I wanted them to also share in our All Talk Math, but the new student preferred to listen only and, in this particular case, I decided to respect that. I know All Talk Math is about all students having the opportunity to say something to the whole class. However, regarding this student, being not only in my class but in the United States for such little time, feeling welcome and respected was more important today. Next time, I need to make sure all students participate. I plan to partner my new emergent multilingual with another student I have who speaks the same language at home. They can rehearse what to say, and that can be translated to English by the partner if we need.

I felt that my math discourse techniques, using Task Think-Aloud to Launch and All Talk Math at the end of the Discuss phase of the lesson, went well overall. Ultimately, most students were successful in their understanding of place value and comparing numbers. They need to be able to better articulate for themselves and others how we go about comparing the numbers. This is hard for them. I will have to think of other numbers to give them to compare that can challenge some of their ideas to clarify the mathematical reason behind how we do this.

I have to say my favorite part was All Talk Math. Students participated and had a voice. As we gathered on the floor, students listened respectfully to each other. Many students shared that when comparing numbers, you look at both numbers, compare the digits in the hundreds place first, the tens second, and the ones last. I also recognized from All Talk Math that students were realizing that numbers go beyond hundreds. I spend so much time talking about ones, tens, and hundreds that students were locked into thinking about numbers with three digits. Thousands, ten thousands—we need to work on that vocabulary!

Examining Ms. Abdal's Discuss Phase

Ms. Abdal uses All Talk Math for students to present a summary of their mathematical understanding of using place value to compare numbers. When using this technique, there are moments when the teacher intervenes to focus students' responses on the question posed. Using All Talk Math as a summary tool, Ms. Abdal hears remaining misunderstandings students have at the conclusion of the lesson that can inform future lessons to address those ideas. Students also get to hear their peers explain their reasoning about how to compare numbers using knowledge of place value.

DISCUSS WITH COLLEAGUES

1   How do you typically encourage participation from your students in whole-group discussions? What have you found that helps engage students who are hesitant to talk in whole-group discussions (about math or other content areas)?

2   What are some ways you can draw on students' prior knowledge during All Talk Math?

3   What should you keep in mind when determining the order in which students share? What are some ways to communicate to students how to follow the order you intend on their own?

CONNECT TO YOUR PRACTICE

Consider using the All Talk Math technique in a Discuss phase to help your students make connections between new ideas from the lesson and previously learned ideas. Plan some questions or prompts and corresponding sentence starters to facilitate this All Talk Math discussion.

NOTES

_____

_____

_____

_____

_____

_____

_____

_____

_____

_____

_____

_____

_____

Probing and Pressing Math Questions

Teachers ask questions throughout the day in every subject area, but some questions are more powerful than others in challenging students to think deeply. In literacy, "skinny questions" are usually closed-ended, requiring brief, factual answers, whereas "fat questions" are open-ended and invite students to share their thinking (Kagan, 1999). When reading with young students, you might ask fat questions to support comprehension and critical thinking or to press students to justify their ideas with evidence from the text. In writing, teachers often ask open-ended questions to help students elaborate on their ideas and add details to their stories. Similarly, the Probing and Pressing Math Questions technique involves asking powerful questions designed to help students go deeper in their thinking about math and to share that thinking with others. Thus, these are fat questions for mathematics.

WHAT ARE PROBING AND PRESSING MATH QUESTIONS?

To understand this technique, you first need to know that in our work, Probing and Pressing Math Questions are not synonymous; they are two distinct types of fat math questions for different purposes. Probing Questions invite students to explain their mathematical thinking in detail, sharing their reasoning or justifying their solutions with more information than originally provided. These questions help students elaborate on their ideas and share more than they might be able to on their own, without teacher support. Pressing Questions challenge students to reason more deeply about key mathematical ideas, seek connections among ideas or solution strategies, and make meaning of their work. Teachers often use a combination of Probing and Pressing Math Questions to support their learning goals for students.

Probing Questions: questions that invite students to explain their mathematical thinking in detail, sharing their reasoning or justifying their solutions with more information than originally provided

Pressing Questions: questions that challenge students to reason more deeply about key mathematical ideas, seek connections among ideas or solution strategies, and make meaning of their work

173

WHY MIGHT YOU USE PROBING AND PRESSING MATH QUESTIONS?

Imagine that your students have been working in pairs to solve a story problem during the Explore phase, and you are ready for a whole-group discussion. When you call on students to share how they approached the problem with the class, their explanations are brief and lacking in depth. They might say, "I added the numbers" or "I drew a picture," but they don't offer details about the reasoning behind their ideas, so it is difficult to engage them in rich math discourse. The Probing and Pressing Math Questions technique is a scaffold for students to help them learn to expand and deepen the explanations they share.

Purposes of Probing and Pressing Math Questions

- Bring forth details of students' mathematical arguments that they might not mention on their own
- Challenge students to think deeply and build mathematical connections
- Encourage students to justify their quantitative reasoning
- Have students use math structures and apply ideas to new problems
- Engage students in sense-making regarding what they are learning

Using the Probing and Pressing Math Questions technique during the Discuss phase supports students in making sense of their learning from the Explore phase, helping them go deeper with their mathematical thinking and share their ideas as part of a math community.

GETTING STARTED WITH PROBING AND PRESSING MATH QUESTIONS

Before using the Probing and Pressing Math Questions technique, make sure to give students enough time to engage with the task so that they are ready to begin sharing their ideas and can benefit from considering how others have approached the task. To implement the Probing and Pressing Math Questions technique, use the following steps:

1. In planning for the lesson, think about what questions you might ask students based on the problem or task selected and the type of information you want students to attend to in their explanations. Examples of questions you might ask for particular purposes are shown in Figure 15-1. Anticipate how students might respond to each question, and think about the kinds of answers you are hoping for, so you are ready to model responses and further scaffold if students are struggling to explain their thinking.

Figure 15-1 ◆ Examples of Probing and Pressing Math Questions

Probing Questions

1 Invite detailed sharing of a solution method:
   - How did you . . . ?
   - Can you show us what it looked like when you . . . ?
2 Prompt students to share reasoning:
   - Why did you decide to . . . ?
   - What made you think that . . . ?
3 Encourage students to justify their solution method or result:
   - How did you know that would work?
   - Is there a way to check if your answer is correct?

Pressing Questions

1 Ask students to connect parts of two or more approaches:
   - Where can we find the 7 in each of these solution methods?
   - How does each solution method show that we are regrouping?
2 Ask students to compare approaches:
   - Why do these two solution methods both work for this problem?
3 Ask students to use a solution approach for a new problem:
   - How would we solve the next problem using the method we just saw?
4 Have students make meaning of their work:
   - How did your solution answer the question asked in the problem?
   - Would your method always work, even with different numbers? How do you know?

Source: Project All Included in Mathematics, North Carolina State University and Horizon Research, Inc. Copyright 2016. Used with permission.

2. As students are working on the task, circulate and notice how different students are approaching the problem. Think about which students you want to share their work with the class, for what purposes you will select each response, and the specific questions you want to ask students.
3. During the Discuss phase, ask Probing and Pressing Math Questions as students share their work with the whole class. Be sure to give sufficient wait time for students to think and respond to your questions.

4. After each student answers a question, give additional wait time for the class to think about and process the ideas that have been shared.

5. Continue asking Probing and Pressing Math Questions throughout the discussion to challenge students to go deeper and carefully consider each other's ideas.

THINK ABOUT IT

Read the examples of Probing and Pressing Math Questions in Figure 15–1 again. What other questions and question starters could you use to help students share their mathematical thinking and reason more deeply?

As you become more comfortable using the Probing and Pressing Math Questions technique, you may find that you naturally start thinking of questions you want to ask students based on the work you see happening in the moment, beyond the questions you have prepared. That's great! This technique is most powerful when you can ask a combination of questions you have carefully planned ahead of time and questions that allow you to take advantage of students' rich, in-the-moment mathematical thinking, even when they're approaching the task in ways you didn't expect.

SUPPORTS THAT HELP WITH PROBING AND PRESSING MATH QUESTIONS

For students to feel comfortable and confident taking risks when sharing their thinking, offering substantial support is critical. There are several scaffolds you can provide during each phase of the lesson to help students feel confident in responding to your questions.

Preview questions. During the Launch phase, let students know the kinds of questions you will ask later. For example, "Everyone should be able to tell me in our discussion if they needed to regroup and why" or "I will ask you later to share with everyone how you decided to solve the problem." Similarly, as you monitor students' work during the Explore phase, let specific students or groups know what kinds of questions you might ask about their work so that they have time to think about and rehearse how to answer it when they present their solution. For example, "I want you to share this picture with the whole class. When you do, I will ask you to explain how you made this picture from the story problem and what it represents. I will also ask you to connect the picture and your solution." Letting students know in advance what questions you will ask is especially important for helping emergent multilingual learners feel comfortable sharing their thinking with the class.

Wait time. Probing and Pressing Math Questions are designed to get students thinking, so give them time to do that. For example, you might let students know directly that you are giving them time to think: "I'm going to ask a question, and I want everyone to think about their own answer quietly before I call on anyone to share." You could also encourage all students to write something down, using pictures, symbols, or words, as they consider the questions.

Sentence starters. Providing sentence starters can give students a starting point to formulate their responses to your questions. Sentence starters like "I decided to use this strategy because . . ." or "I know my solution works because . . ." can help students explain and justify their solution methods. You can tailor the sentence starters to the questions that you ask during the lesson and model the kind of discourse you hope to hear from students.

Math word bank. A math word bank with terms relevant to the lesson or problem can help students expand their responses, adding detail and precision as they share their mathematical thinking with the class.

SIGNS OF SUCCESS

- Students elaborate and share details about their thinking.

- Students explain and value their own ideas, offering reasoning and justification.

- Students make connections among ideas, strategies, and solutions.

CAUTION SIGNALS

- Students give only brief responses. (Say, "Tell me more," and model how to use the sentence starters or other supports to help students share their thinking.)

- Students consistently answer, "I don't know." (Clarify the question if needed, and tell students you are eager to hear their ideas after you give them more time to think.)

IMPROVING AND ADAPTING PROBING AND PRESSING MATH QUESTIONS

The following ideas will support you in extending and going deeper with this technique.

Teach students to ask questions. As students become comfortable responding to your Probing and Pressing Math Questions, you can help them develop their own questioning skills. Begin with Probing Questions and, as the year progresses, you can shift to Pressing Questions. Provide question starters that students can use to ask each other about their mathematical thinking, such as those provided in Figure 15-1. You can also assign the role of questioner to specific students during the discussion of a task. It's important to model using these question starters and guide students in selecting which ones to use rather than having them randomly pick one that might not be appropriate or useful for a certain problem. By teaching students to ask their own questions, you can help them take on greater responsibility as part of the discourse community.

Combine talk techniques. You can combine Probing and Pressing Math Questions with other discourse techniques to support students as they learn to communicate their mathematical thinking with others. For example, after one student responds to a question, you might invite another student to restate the answer in their own words to encourage active listening. You could also have students use the Think-Pair-Rehearse-Share technique (Chapter 9) after posing a question so that all students have an opportunity to think and practice explaining their answers with a partner before sharing with the whole class. If students are working in small groups, you might assign one or two of them the role of questioner, as in the Talk Triangle technique (Chapter 11). Let these students know that they are responsible for asking Probing or Pressing Math Questions of others in their groups, and rotate roles so that each student has an opportunity to practice asking these kinds of questions.

EXAMINE PRACTICE

In this vignette, Ms. Tate-Salina uses Probing and Pressing Math Questions throughout her lesson, modeling what will happen in the Discuss phase. This vignette is a continuation of Ms. Tate-Salina's lesson presented in Chapter 8, and some elements of her planning are repeated. As you read the vignette, ask yourself: Which of the teacher's questions are Probing Questions, and which are Pressing Questions? Consider whether the questions are effective in pushing students to share more or think deeper about the math task.

Probing and Pressing Math Questions in Ms. Tate-Salina's Fourth-Grade Classroom

Planning the Lesson

Multiplicative comparison problems are hard for my fourth-grade students. My goal for the lesson was for students to conceptually understand the anatomy of this type of problem. I chose to use Math Bet Lines in the Launch phase to help students identify the structure of multiplicative comparisons. I also wanted students to work on questioning; this was my overall discourse goal for the lesson. I wanted them to use Probing and Pressing Math Questions when we got to our discussion of these problems. My plan was to model such questions throughout the lesson, referring to question stems I have posted in the room, so students could ask these types of questions of each other later in the Discuss phase.

This is my fourth year teaching fourth grade, and I have built a resource of favorite lessons. For this lesson, I selected two problems in which the multiplier factor is given. I wanted students to be able to compose the correct equation for each problem. I also wanted them to compare the structures of these problems. My plan was for students to list three things they noticed and one thing they wondered about the problems and their structures. After that, I was going to have students solve two other problems that we would address in the Discuss phase.

(continued)

EXAMINE PRACTICE (continued)

> Lake Glenn in Virginia is 55 miles long.
>
> Lake Glenn is 5 times as long as Lake Parker.
>
> How long is Lake Parker?

> Over the summer, José read 9 books.
>
> Rachel read 4 times as many books.
>
> How many books did Rachel read?

This lesson ended up being harder than I had anticipated and did not unfold quite as planned. My students needed more time to think about each problem before they could compare them.

Enacting the Lesson

When I launched the lesson using Math Bet Lines, I realized after the first problem that students were not sure how to solve that problem. Only about half of my 25 students thought that Lake Glenn was longer than Lake Parker. So I let them work on the problem, and then I called them back together for the Discuss phase. I showed students two representations I had noticed around the room and asked what was the difference between them.

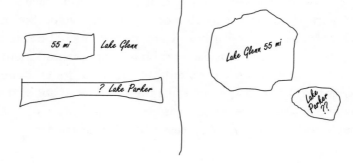

A student answered, "Lake Parker is bigger in this picture than in the other picture," and I revoiced, "On the left, we have someone suggesting that Lake Parker is bigger than Lake Glenn, and on the right another student indicates that Lake Glenn is bigger." I said to students, "If you think, like the picture on the left, that Lake Parker is bigger, tell us why." A few students told the story problem in their own words, emphasizing the "five times" from the story. As I was asking Probing Questions, it became clear that they were thinking the problem was telling them to compute "Lake Glenn five times" to find the length of Lake Parker. Then Jonee disagreed, suggesting that the problem said that Lake Glenn was bigger than the other one, and if we did 55 x 5, it would make the other lake bigger. At that point, I asked, "What is Jonee saying that is different from what you said?" I let the students lead the discussion, and they were really trying to explain their reasons to each other. I kept asking more questions when needed, to try to bring the group to some closure.

When I heard Cameron say, "Lake Glenn is 5 times more than Lake Parker, so if you divide it, you get Lake Parker," I asked him to go up to the board and show where in the story it said it was *more*. He came to the board and wrote $\frac{55}{5}$, explaining in his own words that the problem indicates division. I asked, "Can someone explain why he divided?" and the discussion kept going. Some students highlighted that the problem said *times*; it did not say to *divide*. Cameron argued the problem did not have to tell them what to do; we had to pay attention to the situation. Still, many students wanted to compute 55 x 5, and the discussion continued until Jamila said, "I think the problem is trying to trick you when it says 5 *times* as long as Parker because you might think to multiply, but it is really just saying that Lake Glenn is bigger, like 5 times bigger. So if it is bigger, Lake Parker is smaller, 5 times smaller." At this point, I needed to keep the lesson moving, so I came to the board and said that if Lake Glenn was 5 times the size of Lake Parker, we could write: 5 x P = G or 5 x P = 55, and we worked our way to finding that Lake Parker was 11 miles long.

The Discuss phase continued as I showed students the next problem and asked them how the two problems were different. "Do not solve this second problem. Just read it and think about how it is different from the other one."

(continued)

EXAMINE PRACTICE (continued)

Lake Glenn in Virginia is 55 miles long. Lake Glenn is 5 times as long as Lake Parker. How long is Lake Parker?	Over the summer José read 9 books. Rachel read 4 times as many books. How many books did Rachel read?

How are these two problems different?
Be ready to share your thoughts!

Equation:	Equation:

My students' initial responses showed attention to superficial aspects of the problem, such as "the numbers are different" or "the other problem is about books," so I continued to ask Probing Questions. Clariana then explained that for the new problem, she would multiply to solve. She continued to say that Rachel read more than José and if she divided the numbers, she would get a different answer. Many students agreed with her, so I came up to the board and wrote, for the first problem, 5 x P = 55 and, for the second problem, 4 x 9 = R. When I asked why these were different, many students attended to the order in which the names were said in the story, or how many times the names were said, to decide whether they had to multiply or divide to find the solution. Samir then said, "I see how they are kind of the same, but the lake one they are tricking you into thinking 55 x 5, but the other one they are not tricking you. It's the normal question." I asked, "Why do you call that normal on the new problem?" and Samir explained, "Because it says times and you multiply." I needed to conclude the discussion, and I shared with the students, "You may be used to working with direct problems where you can identify whether to add, or multiply, or divide after your first read of the problem. You will start seeing comparisons given to you in different ways, and you will have to think about the structure of the problem to decide on the equation and then see if you need to multiply or divide to find the answer. But you really have to picture the story to think about this." I guess at this point, at the end of the lesson, students were perhaps thinking at the level where I thought they would be at the start of the lesson!

Reflecting on the Discuss Phase

During this lesson, it became clear to me that my students were not ready to interpret multiplicative comparison problems written in different ways. So I needed to do more work with them on representing and solving the different types of multiplicative comparison problems. But we really made use of discourse supported by Probing and Pressing Math Questions to improve the way we discuss our math problems and think hard about what we are doing. I encouraged students to carry on conversations regarding the math problems at hand in detail and in a respectful manner for the goal of helping them understand the thinking of others. I used a lot of modeling, including referring to the question stems displayed in my classroom, and students asked really good questions. I was satisfied with the quality of our discussions overall, and I think they helped students think further about these types of problems—although we still have work to do regarding multiplicative comparisons.

Examining Ms. Tate-Salina's Discuss Phase

The Probing and Pressing Math Questions Ms. Tate-Salina used in the Discuss phase of the lesson helped students make sense of the mathematical structure of multiplicative comparison problems. Having realized that many students were not understanding how to solve this type of problem and, instead, were focusing on the idea of whether the problem is "tricking" you with key words, the teacher's questioning orchestrates the conversation toward the need to model the situation with math and use this model to decide which operation to use. Ms. Tate-Salina's Discuss phase shows how using Probing and Pressing Math Questions brings the discussion toward the big mathematical ideas of the lesson, even when those ideas were not what she initially planned for.

DISCUSS WITH COLLEAGUES

1   What kinds of questions do you usually ask students during math instruction? Are they mostly open-ended (fat questions), closed-ended (skinny questions), or a combination? How do your students respond to different types of questions?

2   What are some other ideas to support students in answering your Probing and Pressing Math Questions, beyond the ideas described in this chapter? Do you use scaffolds in other subject areas that you can adapt to promote high-quality math discourse in your classroom?

CONNECT TO YOUR PRACTICE

Plan a lesson using the Probing and Pressing Math Questions technique during the Discuss phase. As you plan, write down questions to elicit students' thinking and foster mathematical connections among ideas. Provide one or two sentence starters that could support students in answering your questions. After the lesson, reflect on how the Probing and Pressing Math Questions played out. What was successful? What was challenging?

NOTES

_____

_____

_____

_____

_____

Math Learning Summary

Determining the main idea of a story is one of the most complex reading comprehension skills for students. More often than not, students are able to easily recall concrete facts and details from a story, but identifying the main idea of a passage or the moral of a story is more abstract and challenging. The same can be said for extracting the main idea of a math lesson. Students may be able to tell you what they *did* during math class, but can they tell you what they *learned*? Derived from the language-experience approach used to teach reading and writing (Stauffer, 1970), the Math Learning Summary technique is designed to help students reflect on and make sense of their mathematical learning to solidify their understanding during the Discuss phase of a lesson.

> ## THINK ABOUT IT
>
> How do your students typically engage in sense-making of key mathematical ideas? What instructional strategies have been successful for having students share what they understand?

WHAT IS MATH LEARNING SUMMARY?

The Math Learning Summary technique is a way to engage the whole class in identifying, synthesizing, and articulating the main concepts that emerge from work on a math task or a collection of tasks. With guidance from the teacher, students draw on their shared mathematical experiences from the lesson to co-create a collective record of their learning (e.g., a paragraph, a key sentence or two) during the Discuss phase. This record serves as a product of their shared knowledge and a reference for future lessons. An example of a Math Learning Summary from a second-grade lesson on using place value in subtraction is shown in Scenario 16-1. During this lesson, students were asked to solve a story problem involving numbers between 10 and 90.

Math Learning Summary: a technique that engages the whole class in identifying, synthesizing, and articulating the main concepts that emerge from work on a math task or a collection of tasks

185

Ms. Yang's class donated 67 books to the school book drive. The books were sorted into two piles: picture books and chapter books. Twenty-three books went into the picture book pile. How many books went into the chapter book pile?

The teacher selected three students to present their solution strategies to the whole class. After the class compared and discussed the different strategies, the teacher asked students to create a summary of what they learned about subtraction from the task.

SCENARIO 16-1

OUR MATH LEARNING SUMMARY: SUBTRACTION

When we are subtracting, we can take away different ways. We can take away all or take away one by one. We can decompose some numbers in an equation to make tens that help with taking away. It will be faster to answer questions counting back by tens and ones instead of counting back only by ones. We can also count up by tens and ones from the smaller number if we don't want to take away. That is also faster than counting up by ones.

WHY MIGHT YOU USE MATH LEARNING SUMMARY?

As with the other talk techniques, your decision to use Math Learning Summary depends on the main goal(s) of your lesson. At the start of a unit, you may want students to begin exploring ideas, and they may not yet be ready to consider the broader concepts. Or at times, you may want to focus your lesson on productive practice of facts and procedures. In these cases, using the Math Learning Summary technique may *not* be appropriate. But when the goal of your lesson is to focus on and formalize a specific conceptual idea to promote sense-making, Math Learning Summary is an effective technique to ensure this goal is met. By having students bring together the important content goals of the lesson into a formalized summary, you can make sure big mathematical ideas are explicitly presented for all students in your class.

Purposes of Math Learning Summary

- Articulate main mathematical concepts learned in one or many lessons
- Synthesize various mathematical ideas that have been shared during the lesson(s)
- Document connections among various representations and solution methods
- Look for and express structure(s) across current and previously learned mathematical ideas
- Make mathematical generalizations
- Develop and use precise language to represent students' understanding

Math Learning Summary encourages student engagement in a number of features of the Math Discourse Matrix (Figure 1-2), including mathematical explanations, active listening, student-to-student communication, and connections among different representations as modes of communication about math. Fostering the use of everyday language and developing students' academic language are additional benefits of using this technique.

GETTING STARTED WITH MATH LEARNING SUMMARY

When you first implement the Math Learning Summary technique, use the following steps:

1. Have students participate in a common math learning experience (i.e., exploring a task). Make sure to select a discourse-promoting task (Figure 3-1). After all, the experience with the task serves as the basis for the summary.

2. Before co-creating the summary, ask the whole class to discuss their solution strategies and any mathematical connections that might emerge. Getting out in the open the essential ideas about what students did mathematically first will help them make sense of the math and pull out the key ideas for the summary. Without this step, the summary may become a simple step-by-step recounting of what they *did* during the exploration rather than a synthesis of what they *learned*.

3. Call on students to begin offering sentences describing what they learned about the content of the lesson from the math experience.

4. Record their contributions (in summary format) while asking guiding questions to help draw out important mathematical ideas and to encourage precise statements that will lead to a clear and focused summary. It is important to record students' ideas verbatim to show that their language, whether it is everyday or academic, is accepted and valued. Keeping the focus of the summary on the substance of what students are saying rather than how they are saying it will enable more equitable math learning opportunities. At the same time, make sure that the contributions you record are aligned with the lesson goals.

5. Ask the whole class to read the summary aloud to reinforce the ideas and practice with the language that emerged. You may want to read it first as a model and then have the class read it together, particularly in earlier grades. The collective summary can then be posted in the classroom as a point of reference for future lessons that draw on this shared knowledge.

6. When appropriate to their writing proficiency, ask students to also record the summary in their notes to create a personal record of their learning.

SUPPORTS THAT HELP WITH MATH LEARNING SUMMARY

Synthesizing broad mathematical ideas is a sophisticated way to think, especially for primary-grade students. It requires teacher scaffolding to help students move from thinking about their work on a particular problem (e.g., how they solved a subtraction problem) to the mathematical connections at the center of the experience and the generalizability of that work (e.g., how that solution method applies to other subtraction problems, how the structure of a problem relates to different solution methods). Modeling the difference between summarizing main ideas about the *learning* versus recounting *the process* is key! The following are some other supports that may be helpful:

Guiding questions. Because synthesizing information is difficult, students may share sentences that include both what they did and what they learned, and that's okay! In fact, having students describe what they did on a task might be a good way to get started, and then you can use guiding questions to draw out the key learning points to record for the summary. If students only summarize their steps to solving the problem, you might want to ask:

- *What mathematical ideas did you learn from our exploration?*
- *What mathematical connections did we make today?*

Tailoring prompts to the selected math task will also help target more specific ideas from the exploration. For example:

- *After going through the steps you just shared, what is something new or interesting you realized about . . . ?*
- *Were there any regularities you noticed about . . . and . . . ?*

Questions like these will refocus students' thinking and help them make sense of what they learned, not just recall what they did, through the problem-solving process.

Math word bank. During the Explore phase, you may want to create a word bank of the relevant math language you hear students using so they can refer to it during the Discuss phase when they co-create the summary. The word bank can support language access and promote language production because it collects words from various students that all students can then use.

Sentence starters. Sentence starters may be especially helpful for focusing students' contributions on their learning. Examples of useful sentence starters for Math Learning Summary include "A big idea we learned was . . ., " "A mathematical connection we found was . . .," and "We realized that . . . ." You may also want to include some sentence starters that foster wonderings, questions, or generalizations based on the gained knowledge, like "Our new understanding of . . . makes me wonder . . . ."

Even with these supports, it is important to remember that not all students will feel immediately comfortable contributing to the summary, perhaps due to their limited language proficiency or difficulty in synthesizing information. Giving students independent think time provides everyone with an opportunity to consider an idea to contribute. Students can write down what they might say or rehearse it with a partner, both of which support all students' math communication and can often lead to greater participation in the Math Learning Summary technique.

SIGNS OF SUCCESS

- Students' contributions state precisely something they learned about math in the lesson.

- Students' contributions fit together in a summary that addresses the math learning goal.

- Students use and value everyday and academic language to summarize their learning.

CAUTION SIGNALS

- Students describe only what they did. (Provide sentence starters that help students focus their contributions on what they learned from what they did.)

- Students share only vague statements. (Ask guiding questions that push for more precision.)

- Students are uncertain of the math content of the lesson and struggle to offer ideas for the summary. (Scaffold students' contributions by asking about things you heard and noticed during the Explore phase.)

IMPROVING AND ADAPTING MATH LEARNING SUMMARY

Once you are comfortable with the basic steps of Math Learning Summary, we offer the following recommendations for how to better prepare for and use this technique with students, including ideas for adaptation.

Anticipate how students will respond. Prior to the lesson, anticipate how students will respond to the selected problem or task and how the important mathematical ideas for the lesson may be evident in their work and explanations. Knowing ahead of time what may surface gives you a sense of how the whole-group discussion may transpire and how to more thoughtfully orchestrate the creation of the summary.

Encourage participation in small groups. Use Math Learning Summary when working with a small group of students (e.g., a guided math group) rather than with the whole class. Using this technique in smaller groups is likely to develop students' willingness and confidence in offering ideas and increase their opportunities to participate.

Use with Math Talk Chain. Pair Math Learning Summary with Math Talk Chain (Chapter 13) as a structure for the initial discussion of the shared math learning experience. The two techniques pair nicely, with Math Talk Chain eliciting students' ideas in a connected way and Math Learning Summary helping them synthesize and make sense of those ideas. You and your students may find other ways to pair techniques to accomplish your goals; be creative!

Plan Probing and Pressing Math Questions. Prior to the lesson, plan Probing Questions that will focus students' thinking as well as Pressing Questions to push for mathematical depth (Chapter 15). It is helpful to have these questions written down and easily accessible during the lesson.

Although Math Learning Summary provides opportunities to work on language development, too much focus on language rather than the mathematical ideas may discourage participation. At the same time, you want the summary to be precise. If a student's contribution is vague or difficult for others to understand, ask follow-up questions so the student can provide more focus and clarity. Because the Math Learning Summary is a co-created product for the whole class, another option is to revoice or have students restate one another's contributions as you press for more accessible and/or precise statements.

Math Learning Summary may be challenging to implement the first time or two. Not only does it come at the very end of a lesson when you may be short on time, but it is heavily dependent on students' abilities to extract sophisticated mathematical ideas from a shared learning experience and your ability as their teacher to facilitate and focus their contributions toward broader concepts. As with any other instructional technique, it will become easier over time with more practice, scaffolds, and purposeful planning. Reserving enough time to implement this technique well will pay off for you and your students. Before long, your students will become experts at making meaning of the math they experience in class and creating an ongoing record that registers the main mathematical ideas they have been learning.

EXAMINE PRACTICE

When reading the vignette from Ms. Zara, ask yourself: What did this teacher do throughout the lesson to support the class in creating a Math Learning Summary that synthesized important mathematical ideas the students learned? Consider other ways teachers can support students in creating a precise summary of their key mathematical understandings.

Math Learning Summary in Ms. Zara's Fifth-Grade Classroom

Planning the Lesson

This story represents the first day I worked with my fifth graders on division with fractions. My goal was to introduce the concept of dividing a whole number by a unit fraction and discuss what happens. So I prepared to use clay to represent the number in each group and paper circles to represent the number of groups. Part of my goal was to get students to think open-mindedly and reach conclusions by noticing patterns through their own exploration. I wanted students to examine and synthesize these patterns at the end of the lesson.

My discourse goal for this lesson was for students to collaborate by explaining, listening, and agreeing about how to solve problems. I chose to use Math Bet Lines during the Launch phase to engage students with the problems. Then I wanted to spend most of the lesson on the Explore phase, with students working in small groups to model the problems from the worksheet I had prepared. To conclude the lesson, I planned for a Discuss phase that combined two techniques. I wanted to have an All Talk Math in which all students could share patterns and interesting results and then use Math Learning Summary to bring together students' realizations. My idea was to record what students said in the All Talk Math and use that to co-create the summary.

The worksheet I used had students first predict what the result of $6 \div \frac{1}{3}$ would be. I knew they would think of numbers smaller than 6 for their predictions. Then I had them work on modeling problems like $6 \div 2$, $6 \div 1$, and $6 \div \frac{1}{2}$ with clay. I wanted them to model each problem considering the divisor as the number of groups or as the number per group. At the end, I asked them to examine what happened as the divisor got smaller. In my 17 years of teaching, I have seen again and again that division by fractions is hard. I want my students to have powerful ways to think about it and model it.

Enacting the Lesson

My 19 students were organized in groups of 3 or 4 during the Launch phase, when we revisited the different types of division problems. Then they transitioned to the Explore phase and started working on the worksheet problems, while I circulated to support the various groups. When they got to $6 \div \frac{1}{2}$, I had students first consider that $\frac{1}{2}$ was the number in each group and so we needed to give $\frac{1}{2}$ of one whole to each group, using all 6 wholes. This led students to create 12 groups. Students were saying they needed more groups because they divided each of their clay balls, which represented 1, into halves. That was cool. Then I had them consider what it would mean when $\frac{1}{2}$ was the number of groups. They really paused to think about this suggestion. But then students in many of the small groups folded or cut their circles in half to create a "half group," and once they had the 6 clay balls in there for a half group, I asked how many would be in a whole group, which got them back to the same answer of 12.

After about 40 minutes, I had students clear their desks, and we engaged in All Talk Math so that students could share their observations about the problems we had worked on. Not all statements were about division by unit fractions, but some of the interesting ones included ideas like these:

- *The answers get bigger rather than smaller.*
- *When the divisor gets smaller, the quotient gets bigger.*
- *If you multiply the whole number by the denominator, you get the quotient when dividing a whole number by a fraction.*
- *Checking with the inverse gets you the same answer.*

(continued)

EXAMINE PRACTICE (continued)

I wrote those statements on the board and moved on to work on the Math Learning Summary. Before the lesson, I created a structure for the summary that I wanted students to use, which I put on the white board to get started:

Today . . .

First we . . .

Then . . .

We found out . . .

This reminds us that . . .

One of my students volunteered to start our class summary with "Today in math class at our school, " which I wrote down. Then we talked about the goal of the lesson, which ended with the statement:

Today in math class at our school, we learned how to divide a whole number by a unit fraction.

I encouraged students to think through what we had done in class, and the summary continued:

First we used clay to make wholes and paper circles to make groups. Then we put the clay dividend in our division box. After that we divided the dividend (clay) into groups (circles) based on the divisor.

Because I wanted students to think about the big ideas of the lesson, not the mechanics of what we had done, I tried to point them to what was on the board from our All Talk Math. We then added a precise statement of an idea to our summary:

We found out that when your divisor is less than one, the quotient became bigger than the dividend.

Before writing the final sentence about what this reminded us of, I brought students' attention back to the prediction they had at the beginning of class about the quotient of $6 \div \frac{1}{3}$. All of the students had predicted a quotient that was less than 6, which is how they are used to thinking about division. When I encouraged them to think about what happened when they multiplied a whole number by a number less than one (the product got smaller) and then what happened when dividing by a unit fraction, we concluded the Math Learning Summary:

> *Today in math class at our school, we learned how to divide a whole number by a unit fraction. First we used clay to make wholes and paper circles to make groups. Then we put the clay dividend in our division box. After that we divided the dividend (clay) into groups (circles) based on the divisor. We found out that when your divisor is less than one, the quotient became bigger than the dividend. This reminds us that operating with fractions changes other numbers in unexpected ways.*

Reflecting on the Discuss Phase

Overall, I was pleased with the final summary. We have been doing quite a bit of work with writing summaries in language arts, and it has been useful to develop main ideas and concepts and to reach closure of a lesson in a math class as well. I was also glad we could add some precision to our language during the summary time.

Luisa, my new emergent multilingual learner, had trouble participating in this summary exercise, so I know I will go back and revisit the summary with her and a few other students tomorrow. During the lesson, I paired Luisa with a peer who is a very collaborative math student and speaks both Spanish and English well—that helped and they worked well together on the math. During All Talk Math, Luisa repeated what someone else said, so perhaps next time she can prepare and rehearse what she wants to share before we start the discussion. Still, I am pretty sure she understood the math concept from the lesson, and I will make sure the summary made sense to her.

Overall, I think my students needed more time to develop the summary well. This was our first time working on Math Learning Summary, and I could

(continued)

EXAMINE PRACTICE (continued)

have used more time. I could have skipped All Talk Math to save time if I had registered on the white board things that I heard during the facilitation of the small groups. But because I did not do that, I used All Talk Math to collect some ideas for students to use in the summary. All in all, I think the main mathematical idea got across: When we divide by unit fractions or any divisor less than one, the quotient is bigger than the dividend. I am glad my students now have the summary of that idea in their notebooks.

Examining Ms. Zara's Discuss Phase

Ms. Zara combines All Talk Math with Math Learning Summary in the Discuss phase of the lesson to make sure several key mathematical ideas are raised, which can then be added with precision to the shared summary. The teacher is focused on both precision and key ideas, helping students move from sharing the mechanics of the procedures carried out in solving problems to recording the broader mathematical realizations of the lesson. The co-created Math Learning Summary, recorded in students' notebooks, expresses regularities that make mathematical sense and that students can continue to use as their understanding of the math topic unfolds.

DISCUSS WITH COLLEAGUES

1   Consider the modes of communication from the Math Discourse Matrix (Figure I-2). How do you use academic and everyday language, including various first languages for emergent multilingual learners, to develop mathematical reasoning in your class? How can those uses of language help with Math Learning Summary?

2   What aspect of the Math Learning Summary technique do you think will be most challenging to facilitate? What can you do in your planning to help overcome that challenge? And what scaffolds can help your students overcome that challenge?

CONNECT TO YOUR PRACTICE

Plan a lesson using Math Learning Summary in the Discuss phase. Prior to the lesson, write your own summary of the key ideas (maybe three) you want your students to understand from the lesson. After the lesson, review the Math Learning Summary your students created. How can you use it to inform your follow-up instruction?

NOTES

_____

_____

_____

_____

_____

_____

_____

_____

_____

_____

_____

_____

_____

_____

_____

_____

KEY TAKEAWAYS ABOUT THE DISCUSS PHASE

During the Discuss phase, teachers release responsibility for responsive discourse, scaffold engagement, promote students' mathematical authority, and assess students' mathematical understanding. Part V presented four talk techniques (Math Talk Chain, All Talk Math, Probing and Pressing Math Questions, and Math Learning Summary) teachers use to bring their lesson to closure, realizing what was learned. Here are the main takeaways from the chapters:

- Be prepared and flexible, while remaining focused on the mathematical horizon. Lessons do not unfold perfectly; they have detours and unexpected new sights.

- Use the talk techniques to open up your Discuss phase and make your students' mathematical reasoning and arguments available for critique.

- Listen carefully to your students during their discussions to understand what made sense to them and what needs further work; when needed, plan to revisit some math topics later.

- Attend to your emergent multilingual learners and build on their assets to make them integral participants in your math discourse community during the Discuss phase.

Putting It All Together

The Math Discourse Matrix (Figure 1-2). The Math Teaching Guide (Figure 5-1). The 11 talk techniques and additional instructional moves (Figure 4-2) and practices (Figure 4-3). Over the course of this book, we have introduced these discourse resources and tools as a way to activate math talk in your classroom. Now, how do you put them all together? And more importantly, how do you do so purposefully and effectively? The final chapter ties everything together through two more important phases of the lesson: Plan and Reflect. It also offers further suggestions for applying the theoretical ideas and techniques shared in this book to one's own classroom. We will see you at the finish line!

Planning and Reflecting to Promote High-Quality Discourse

Throughout this book, you have taken a journey toward activating math talk in your elementary classroom. In Parts I and II, we set the stage by providing foundational ideas about what constitutes high-quality discourse for all students, the type of math knowledge teachers need to elicit this type of discourse from their students, and how to establish socio-mathematical norms and organize lessons that support productive discussions. Building on that foundation, we described and illustrated 11 purposeful talk techniques, situated within phases of a lesson, that teach students *how* to engage in high-quality discourse for conceptual learning. To help you take that next step and tie all of these ideas together, let's take a closer look at what planning an effective lesson aimed at responsive discourse in your classroom entails.

THE KEY IS IN THE PLANNING

Hopefully you have tried some of the talk techniques in your classroom and are starting to envision, if not already seeing evidence of, what your classroom can look and sound like as your students engage in productive math conversations. Remember, the talk techniques presented in this book are effective only if selected for a particular and appropriate purpose tied to your content and discourse goals. Imagine, if you will, a toolbox. When choosing which tool to use for a particular job, you first need to consider the end goal and then select the tool based on the job that needs to be performed. For instance, if you want to mount a picture frame on the wall, you would most likely grab a hammer and nails rather than a saw to get the job done efficiently and effectively. The same thinking can be applied to teaching. Teachers first identify the math and discourse goals for their lesson and then purposefully select appropriate tasks and techniques to productively address those goals and decide how the lesson will unfold.

The key to all of this is in the planning. As introduced in Chapter 5, the Plan phase of the Math Teaching Guide (Figure 5-1) is essential to the effectiveness of any lesson. The point of this chapter is not to teach you *how* to plan a lesson, but rather to help you think more critically about *what* is planned and how to be more intentional in your decision making when focusing on high-quality discourse.

Over the years, lesson planning tools have been developed to assist teachers in designing effective math lessons. Similarly, our work offers a tool for planning and reflecting on math lessons aimed at promoting responsive discourse. Adapted from "Thinking Through a Lesson Protocol" (M. Smith, Bill, & Hughes, 2008), Figure 17-1 serves as a planning guide that offers important considerations for designing and implementing lessons that promote responsive discourse. The 20 questions, categorized by main lesson components (e.g., setting goals, launching the task, discussing the math), are meant to encourage intentionality in planning around targeted math content and discourse goals.

Preparing for Responsive Discourse: 20 Questions to Ask Yourself: a planning guide that offers important considerations for designing and implementing lessons aimed at promoting responsive discourse

Figure 17-1 ◆ Preparing for Responsive Discourse: 20 Questions to Ask Yourself

As you plan your math lessons aimed at promoting responsive discourse, think carefully about each of the following questions:

A. **Setting Math Content and Discourse Goals**
1. What are my math content goals for this lesson?
2. What are my math discourse goals for this lesson in terms of questioning, explaining, listening, and modes of communication? (Note: Depending on your students' discourse skills, you may not have a goal for each dimension in any one lesson.)

B. **Selecting a Task for Promoting Responsive Discourse**
3. What math task will my students engage with in the lesson? (Note: Always solve the task before deciding to use it.)
4. How does the task address my math content and discourse goals?
5. In which ways is this task discourse-promoting for all students, or how can I adapt it to become discourse-promoting?

C. **Launching the Task**
6. What are my main purposes in launching the selected task?
7. What contextual features, mathematical ideas, or discourse expectations do I need to introduce or scaffold during the Launch phase to make sure all students, including emergent multilingual learners, are ready to engage with the task? (Note: Make sure the Launch phase does not make the task less discourse-promoting.)
8. Given my purposes and the support my students need, what technique can I use to launch the task effectively?

D. **Exploring the Task and Rehearsing to Share**
9. What are my main purposes for the Explore phase?
10. What will I be looking and listening for in the Explore phase to know whether students are meeting the lesson's math content and discourse goals?
11. How will I organize and group students to strengthen their participation in responsive discourse?
12. What questions might I ask, and what resources and scaffolds might I provide, to make sure all students, including emergent multilingual learners, remain actively engaged with the math and are participating through questioning, explaining, listening, and modes of communication?
13. How can I support students in rehearsing the mathematical solutions and ideas they will share in the Discuss phase?
14. Given my purposes and the support my students need, what technique can I use during the Explore phase?

E. **Discussing and Making Sense of the Math**
15. What are my main purposes for the Discuss phase?
16. What structures will I use to make sure all students, including emergent multilingual learners, are taking responsibility for engaging in productive mathematical discussions?
17. What key mathematical ideas, academic language, representations, and connections among solutions do I want to make sure emerge during the Discuss phase?
18. Which anticipated student solutions will be shared during the Discuss phase, and in what order, to get at the key ideas and connections? (Note: Consider how incorrect or incomplete solutions might also be shared to address the math content goals.)
19. What are good questions I can ask to help make students' thinking available to others; to make connections among ideas and representations; and to ensure all my students, including emergent multilingual learners, make sense of key mathematical ideas? (Note: Carefully plan questions about incorrect solutions by raising key ideas without making students feel uneasy.)
20. Given my purposes and the support my students need, what technique can I use during the Discuss phase?

Adapted from M. Smith, Bill, & Hughes (2008).

Initially, the Questions to Ask Yourself might appear somewhat overwhelming and impractical. This protocol, however, is not meant to be used for every lesson, nor are teachers expected to write out formal responses to each of the questions. The intention behind this tool is to help teachers strengthen a mindset of considering these important ideas as they plan their math lessons, in particular when they want students to engage in high-quality math discourse for conceptual learning and procedural fluency. Even if teachers already think of these ideas, the protocol can foster critical and purposeful consideration over time.

THINK ABOUT IT

What questions do you currently ask yourself during lesson planning? How are the Questions to Ask Yourself similar to or different from other lesson-planning tools or resources you may have used in the past? How can you incorporate this tool into your current lesson-planning routine?

REFLECTING TO GROW AND IMPROVE YOUR DISCOURSE PRACTICE

Just as planning is important at the front end of a lesson, reflecting is important at the back end. Reflection is a necessary step in improving one's own practice and further supporting student learning. As presented earlier, the Reflect phase of the Math Teaching Guide (Figure 5-1) pushes teachers to examine their own teaching, review the nature of student engagement, assess student understandings, evaluate progress, and consider further structures for scaffolding and supports.

In the spirit of reflection, take a few moments to think about what you have learned from this book and how it has influenced your math discourse practices thus far.

1. How is your math discourse instruction different as a result of the ideas presented in this book?
2. What about activating math talk has been relatively easy? What aspects continue to be challenging? Why?

Considering questions such as these pushes you to not only analyze your own practice (e.g., identifying strengths and limitations), but also take necessary steps to modify and improve your practice to better support all students.

DISCUSS WITH COLLEAGUES

1   How has your thinking about the planning and implementation of math lessons to promote responsive discourse for all students, including emergent multilingual learners, changed as a result of reading this book?

2   Which talk techniques have helped (or do you think will help) all of your students, especially emergent multilingual learners and emergent math communicators, engage in productive mathematical discussions? In what ways?

3   Which talk techniques have been (or are likely to be) the most challenging for you and your students? What would help you and your students overcome those challenges?

CONNECT TO YOUR PRACTICE

Plan a math lesson that purposefully incorporates at least one talk technique to address a specific discourse goal. Use the Questions to Ask Yourself (Figure 17-1) to guide your lesson planning. After enacting the lesson, reflect on these questions:

☐ How did the lesson play out to address your math content and discourse goals for all your students?

☐ How did the talk technique(s) scaffold and support math discourse for all students, including emergent multilingual learners and emergent math communicators?

☐ How did the planning experience influence the overall nature and quality of the lesson?

☐ How could you further improve this planning process for future lessons?

NOTES

_____

_____

KEY TAKEAWAYS ABOUT PUTTING IT ALL TOGETHER

This final chapter, focused on the Plan and Reflect phases of the Math Teaching Guide, highlighted the importance of this "behind the scenes" work to promote student engagement in high-quality discourse. Here are the main takeaways from the chapter:

- Careful planning and critical reflection are two essential steps toward activating math talk in your classroom.

- Select appropriate instructional tasks, tools, techniques, and scaffolds based on your identified math and discourse goals for the lesson.

- Analyze your own instruction and your students' mathematical understandings to improve practice and student learning.

CONTINUING THE JOURNEY TOWARD HIGH-QUALITY DISCOURSE

Activating math talk in the classroom is not an easy feat, nor does it happen overnight. It is a process that requires knowledge of high-quality math discourse and an understanding of how to organize lessons and purposefully use techniques that scaffold student engagement in communicating their ideas, justifying their reasoning, listening to and questioning others' thinking, and making mathematical connections. It also takes time, practice, and patience. We started our professional development work with elementary teachers over a decade ago with the hope of supporting them in their journey toward promoting more responsive discourse in their classrooms. We have seen teachers transform their instruction and we know it can happen.

Remember—the talk techniques presented in this book are helpful steps toward a larger goal of students engaging in productive math conversations that lead to conceptual learning and procedural fluency. As this part of the journey comes to an end, we encourage you to continue to think about and use the tools and resources provided in this book to improve mathematical discussions in your classrooms and make responsive discourse a reality for your students. We believe you and your students will rise to the challenge and enjoy communicating about math in new and powerful ways.

References

Ball, D. L., Thames, M. H., & Phelps, G. (2008). Content knowledge for teaching: What makes it special? *Journal of Teacher Education, 59,* 389–407.

Brunn, M. (2002). The four-square strategy. *The Reading Teacher, 55,* 522–525.

Carpenter, T., Lindquist, M., Matthews, W., & Silver, E. (1983). Results of the Third NAEP Mathematics Assessment: Secondary school. *The Mathematics Teacher, 76,* 652–659.

Chapin, S. H., O'Connor, M. C., & Anderson, N. (2009). *Classroom discussions: Using math talk to help students learn, grades K–6* (2nd ed.). Sausalito, CA: Math Solutions.

Davey, B. (1983). Think-aloud: Modeling the cognitive processes of reading comprehension. *Journal of Reading, 27,* 44–47.

Dick, L., White, T. F., Trocki, A., Sztajn, P., Heck, D., & Herrema, K. (2016). Supporting sense making with mathematical bet lines. *Teaching Children Mathematics, 22,* 538–545.

Driscoll, M., Heck, D., & Malzahn, K. (2012). Knowledge for teaching English language learners mathematics: A dilemma. In S. Celedón-Pattichis & N. G. Ramirez (Eds.), *Beyond good teaching: Advancing mathematics education for ELLs* (pp. 163–181). Reston, VA: National Council of Teachers of Mathematics.

Hiebert, J., Morris, A. K., & Glass, B. (2003). Learning to learn to teach: An "experiment" model for teaching and teacher preparation in mathematics. *Journal of Mathematics Teacher Education, 6,* 201–222.

Kaddoura, M. (2013). Think pair share: A teaching learning strategy to enhance students' critical thinking. *Educational Research Quarterly, 36,* 3–24.

Kagan, M. (1999). *Higher-level thinking questions.* San Clemente, CA: Author.

Kazemi, E. (1998). Discourse that promotes conceptual understanding. *Teaching Children Mathematics, 4,* 410–414.

Luxford, H., & Smart, L. (2009). *Learning through talk: Developing learning dialogues in the primary classroom.* Abingdon, UK: Routledge.

Lyman, F. (1981). The responsive classroom discussion. In A. S. Anderson (Ed.), *Mainstreaming digest: A collection of faculty and student papers* (pp. 109–113). College Park: University of Maryland College of Education.

Mandel Morrow, L. (1985). Retelling stories: A strategy for improving young children's comprehension, concept of story structure, and oral language complexity. *Elementary School Journal, 85,* 646–661.

McEwan, E. K. (2007). *40 ways to support struggling readers in content classrooms, grades 6–12.* Thousand Oaks, CA: Corwin.

National Council of Teachers of Mathematics. (2014). *Principles to actions: Ensuring mathematical success for all.* Reston, VA: Author.

National Research Council. (2001). *Adding it up: Helping children learn mathematics.* Washington, DC: National Academies Press.

Smith, L. A. (2006). Think-aloud mysteries: Using structured, sentence-by-sentence text passages to teach comprehension strategies. *The Reading Teacher, 59*, 764–773.

Smith, M., Bill, V., & Hughes, E. (2008). Thinking through a lesson protocol: A key for successfully implementing high-level tasks. *Mathematics Teaching in the Middle School, 14*, 132–138.

Smith, M. S., & Stein, M. K. (1998). Selecting and creating mathematical tasks: From research to practice. *Mathematics Teaching in the Middle School, 3*, 344–350.

Smith, M. S., & Stein, M. K. (2018). *5 practices for orchestrating productive mathematics discussions* (2nd ed.). Reston, VA: National Council of Teachers of Mathematics.

Soto-Hinman, I., & Hetzel, J. (2009). *The literacy gaps: Bridge-building strategies for English language learners and standard English learners.* Thousand Oaks, CA: Corwin.

Stauffer, R. G. (1970). *The language-experience approach to the teaching of reading.* New York, NY: Harper & Row.

Thames, M. H., & Ball, D. L. (2010). What mathematical knowledge does teaching require? Knowing mathematics in and for teaching. *Teaching Children Mathematics, 17*, 220–225.

Tompkins, G., Campbell, R., Green, D., & Smith, C. (2014). *Literacy for the 21st century.* Melbourne: Pearson Australia.

Van de Walle, J. A., Karp, K. S., & Bay-Williams, J. M. (2018). *Elementary and middle school mathematics: Teaching developmentally* (10th ed.). Upper Saddle River, NJ: Pearson.

Yackel, E., & Cobb, P. (1996). Socio-mathematical norms, argumentation and autonomy in mathematics. *Journal for Research in Mathematics Education, 27*, 458–477.

Young, C., & Rasinski, T. (2009). Implementing readers theatre as an approach to classroom fluency instruction. *The Reading Teacher, 63*, 4–13.

Index

ALL students should have the opportunity to be successful in mathematics!

Trusted experts in mathematics education offer clear and practical guidance to help students move from surface to deep mathematical understanding, from procedural to conceptual learning, and from rote memorization to true comprehension. Through books, videos, consulting, and online tools, we offer a truly blended learning experience that helps you demystify mathematics for students.

JOHN HATTIE, DOUGLAS FISHER, NANCY FREY, LINDA M. GOJAK, SARA DELANO MOORE, WILLIAM MELLMAN

The what, when, and how of teaching practices that evidence shows work best for student learning in mathematics.

Grades K–12

JOHN ALMARODE, DOUGLAS FISHER, JOSEPH ASSOF, SARA DELANO MOORE, KATERI THUNDER, JOHN HATTIE, NANCY FREY

In this sequel to the best-selling *Visible Learning for Mathematics*, these grade-banded companions show Visible Learning strategies in action in Grades K–2, 3–5, 6–8, and high school mathematics classrooms.

Grades K–2, 3–5, 6–8, and High School

BETH MCCORD KOBETT, RUTH HARBIN MILES, LOIS A. WILLIAMS

Plan math lessons that enhance the purpose, rigor, and coherence of state standards and address the unique learning needs of your individual students.

Grades K–2, 3–5, and 6–8

JOHN SANGIOVANNI, JENNIFER ROSE NOVAK

Armed with hundreds of standards-aligned mathematics tasks and analysis of student work, this series helps you identify misconceptions, fill in common learning gaps, and decide your next instructional moves.

Grades K–2, 3–5, and 6–8

A SAGE Publishing Company

CORWIN HAS ONE MISSION: to enhance education through intentional professional learning.

We build long-term relationships with our authors, educators, clients, and associations who partner with us to develop and continuously improve the best evidence-based practices that establish and support lifelong learning.